Stanislavski in Practice: Exercises for Students

Stanislavski in Practice is an unparalleled, step-by-step guide to Stanislavski's system. Author Nick O'Brien makes this cornerstone of acting accessible to teachers and students alike.

This is an exercise book for students and a lesson planner for teachers on syllabi from Edexcel, WJEC and AQA to the practice-based requirements of BTEC. Each element of the system is covered practically through studio exercises and jargon-free discussion.

Over a decade's experience of acting and teaching makes O'Brien perfectly placed to advise anyone wanting to understand or apply Stanislavski's system.

Features include:

- practical extension work for students to take away from the lesson;
- notes for teachers on how to use material with different age groups;
- exam tips for students based on specific syllabus requirements;
- a chapter dedicated to using Stanislavski when rehearsing a text;
- a glossary of terms that students of the system will encounter.

Nick O'Brien runs Stanislavski workshops across the UK. He trained at the Academy of the Science of Acting and Directing and has a PGCE from Keele University. He is an Examiner for Edexcel.

Stanislavski in Practice: Exercises for Students

NICK O'BRIEN

Routledge
Taylor & Francis Group

LONDON AND NEW YORK

First published 2011
by Routledge
2 Park Square, Milton Park, Abingdon, Oxon OX14 4RN

Simultaneously published in the USA and Canada
by Routledge
711 Third Avenue, New York, NY 10017, USA

Routledge is an imprint of the Taylor & Francis Group, an informa business

Typeset in Charter and Folio by
Florence Production Ltd, Stoodleigh, Devon

British Library Cataloguing in Publication Data
A catalogue record for this book is available from the British Library

Library of Congress Cataloging in Publication Data
O'Brien, Nick, 1972–.
  Stanislavski in practice: exercises for students/Nick O'Brien.
     p. cm.
  Includes index.
  1. Method acting.   2. Acting.   3. Stanislavsky, Konstantin,
  1863–1938.   I. Title.
  PN2062.O27 2010
  792.02'8 – dc22   2010008409

ISBN10: 0–415–56843–9 (pbk)
ISBN10: 0–203–84805–5 (ebk)

ISBN13: 978–0–415–56843–2 (pbk)
ISBN13: 978–0–203–84805–0 (ebk)

FOR MARCUS AND LILLIA

Contents

9 Rehearsing a play   133

10 Improvisations   151

11 The acting exercise programme   158

Figures

Tables

Acknowledgements

Were it not for the 'investment' made by my parents in my training, this book would never have existed and for that I am continually grateful.

My thanks go to Mayumi Ogiwara for receiving my rays and transmitting them into wonderfully clear illustrations, Constance Greenfield and Amber Savva for all their help along the way.

To Thomas Conway for his honest commentary; Patricia O'Brien for checking my homework at school, my dissertation at university and now tirelessly checking drafts of my first book; Matthew Cooper for his camera work; Annie Sutton, Sally Cancello and Victoria May at The Stanislavski Experience; and to Barry Young, Jenni Lewis, Alison Marshall, Sarah Swidenbank and Siobhan Dunne.

My thanks also to Talia Rodgers, Ben Piggott, Niall Slater and Tom Church at Routledge for their help in taking the book from the germ of an idea to what it is now.

And to all the students, teachers and actors I have worked with over the years and to my tutor, the late Sam Kogan.

And finally, to my wife, for putting up with all my newly found writer's eccentricities.

The author and publishers would like to thank the following for their kind permission:

- The Phillips Collection, Washington DC, for the use of Renoir's *Luncheon of the Boating Party;*
- The National Galleries of Scotland for Roy Lichtenstein's *In the Car;*
- The National Gallery of Art in Washington for *Two Women at a Window,* Bartolome Esteban Murillo, and *A Young Girl Reading,* Jean-Honoré Fragonard;
- The Butler Institute of American Art for *Lincoln the Railsplitter*, Norman Rockwell;
- Penguin Books for use of an extract from Chekhov's *The Seagull,* translated by Elisaveta Fen;
- A&C Black Publishers Ltd for the use of an extract from Terry Johnson's *Hysteria;*
- Oxford University Press for use of two extracts from Ibsen's *A Doll's House.*

Introduction

BEFORE YOU START

If you are reading this book, the chances are you're either in the sixth form, or at college, university or drama school. Maybe you are starting your AS year, about to embark on the International Baccalaureate or in the first year of your undergraduate studies.

Acting, by its nature, is all about 'doing', and to understand how to act you must be prepared to 'do'. All the exercises and improvisations in this book are designed with this in mind – to be practised and experienced. If simply read, these exercises will often not be understood, because your understanding will come with practice. So, I ask that you read each exercise, and then you 'give it a go'.

Stanislavski envisaged his system being passed on from actor to actor, from teacher to student, in the form of exercises and improvisations that had evolved and developed in the studios of the Moscow Art Theatre. This book is a continuation of that tradition. It is a collection of exercises and improvisations that have been updated to suit the twenty-first-century drama student and teacher.

Stanislavski developed his system from his work as an actor, director and teacher. His system is a flexible guide for the student to explore and experience a character in preparation for a performance. The Stanislavski system was never intended to be rigid and should not be taken as so. The system evolved and developed over the course of Stanislavski's life, and this book will draw on exercises from Stanislavski's early life as an actor right up to his days at the Opera-Dramatic Studio in Moscow and beyond.

WHERE THE IDEAS AND EXERCISES IN THIS BOOK CAME FROM

A few years ago, I set up a company, The Stanislavski Experience. The company visits schools, colleges and universities, running workshops, initially on Stanislavski, but now on Berkoff, Brecht, devising theatre, physical theatre and directing. The idea behind the company was to deliver practical workshops to help the student understand and experience a practitioner, to give a taste of life at the Moscow Art Theatre or the Berliner Ensemble. We often say in workshops, 'you cannot really understand the Stanislavski system until you use, experience and practise the Stanislavski system.'

I have run workshops from Edinburgh to Guernsey, Somerset to Suffolk, developing and designing exercises and improvisations specifically for the post-16 student. The exercises that appear in this book are taken from a variety of sources and, in most cases, they have been updated and modified to suit the post-16 courses available. Many of these exercises have evolved as I have toured the country delivering Stanislavski workshops; they are the product of what I have found works best in the drama studio with students. Many of the original ideas for exercises are Stanislavski's own, and, as a drama school student, I was lucky enough to train under the late Sam Kogan, by whom I was introduced to many of Stanislavski's exercises first hand. Sam Kogan was tutored by Maria Knebel, one of Stanislavski's pupils and associates, and I feel privileged to be able to pass on to students exercises and ideas passed down through such an esteemed lineage. These exercises, like the system, are not gospel, but offer ways into understanding and experiencing the Stanislavski system.

This book takes the student and teacher through the key areas of the system and on to the rehearsal process. You will be introduced to Stanislavski through exercises that will enable you to understand, through experiencing, the system. Once you have a foundation of practical knowledge, built on real experience and understanding, it is then time for you

Figure i.1
Nick O'Brien

to look in depth at the theory. I often tell students that, really, Stanislavski wanted to make the actor's life easier. By evolving a system, he gave the actor a direction to go in, a path to follow that would lead to truthful acting. Stanislavski wanted us to experience, and, through experiencing, we learn. This book will give you, the student, an experience that will lead you to understand the system and enjoy it.

Many of these exercises, in truth, could appear in a number of different chapters. The system exists, not as stand-alone components, but in harmony as a collective. Therefore, an exercise on objectives can also be on action, imagination and tempo-rhythm. I have split the exercises into areas of the system to aid you in locating their primary purpose.

Recently, there has been a new translation of Stanislavski's work by Jean Benedetti. The new translation, for many, paints a truer picture of Stanislavski's ideas. When I first read *An Actor's Work* (a combination of the old *An Actor Prepares* and *Building a Character*), I could hear, word for word, lessons from my old principal, Sam Kogan. Whole sentences that had been passed from Stanislavski to Maria Knebel and then on to Sam Kogan were, for me, brought alive again through the new translation. This book is designed to work in conjunction with *An Actor's Work*. You do the exercises in a chapter, say on imagination, and then you pick up the original texts and read the correlating chapter. Then, you can read Stanislavski's own words having already gained a practical understanding of that element of the system.

Stanislavski wanted his actors to experience a role actively, and, in that sense, there is always an element of the experimental in his work. In essence, the Stanislavski system is an ongoing process to create believable and truthful characters who harness their imaginations actively.

For you, the student of drama, the Stanislavski system is a guide to help you to experience the role, and, by going through this process, you will understand what many would argue is the foundation stone of acting today.

Stanislavski, in *My Life in Art*, offered us some useful advice:

> If it cannot be mastered immediately then it has to be done in stages, so to speak, put it all together out of individual elements. If each of them has to be worked on separately, systematically, by a whole range of exercises so be it![1]

HOW TO USE THIS BOOK

For the student

This book is divided into chapters outlining the key areas of the system, with the majority of exercises being student exercises, with some that can be led by a group leader or your teacher. At the start of each chapter, there are definitions of the area of the system you will be working on. The majority of exercises have a follow-on exercise for you to practise at home. There are notes for you on each exercise, and exam, performance and rehearsal tips. The improvisations in this book will give you the opportunity to tackle adult characters in a variety of circumstances. This is in preparation for your work on Nina and Kostia, Nora and Torvald, Frank and Rita, George and Martha or Stanley and Blanche. If you are on an IB Theatre Diploma or BTEC National course, this book provides you with a complete framework for your written journals and evaluations.

The exercises throughout the book can be used to support and enhance your studio activities. You can work through the book over the two years of the course doing five or ten minutes here or there, knowing that the skills you are practising have been used by some of the great actors over the last 100 years. Those of you thinking of auditioning for drama school and university drama courses the exercises will give you a grounded technique to use during the audition process. The extension acting exercises (Chapter 11) will help you to gain solid reference points to take with you.

For you, as a student of drama, the book allows you to reflect on classroom exercises and to follow extension tasks designed to improve your understanding. It is the follow-on exercises and your evaluations of the work done in class, that will cement your knowledge and understanding of the system. The book will help you to build confidence and give you an arsenal of skills to draw upon as you develop and mature as an actor.

With the Stanislavski system came an acting vocabulary for all of us to use. The first time I use a specific acting term it will be written in **bold**, so you know that term is a Stanislavski system specific term. A definition of that term will be given in a box to the side of where the term has first been used. In the glossary at the back of this book there will also be a definition for each of these terms for you to read.

I have ordered the chapters in a way I believe best helps you to progress through the system. With each chapter, you will add more skills to the ones you have already learned, building towards chapters on the rehearsal process, improvisations and extension acting exercises where you can test out all your new skills. As you go through each chapter, think about adding the new area of the system to the ones already practised. Each exercise works as part of a chapter or as a stand-alone exercise, so you can work through the whole book systematically or dip in and out of exercises to support your studio activities.

At the end of each of the first eight chapters, you will find a summary box outlining the key areas of the system you have experienced in that chapter. This is to help you consolidate all that you have practised and learned in that chapter.

Ultimately, this book can stay with you throughout your journey as an actor, so in ten years' time, as you are sitting in your dressing room preparing to 'go on', you flick to the chapter on free body and remind yourself of the relaxation exercise.

A couple of years ago, I was coaching a student through her LAMDA exams; she was working on Nina from *The Seagull*. We had worked on the various areas of the system, and she, slowly over the weeks, built her character. She was always concerned with the detail, talking through her objective, clarifying her actions, analysing the events and facts of her character's before-time. Then, the week before the exam, she showed me the piece. I remember watching and thinking, 'Ah, that's what Nina's really like'. For me, that day, I saw a student truly experience the role; she was relaxed, yet active, and completely immersed in 'I am being Nina'. For those few minutes, what Nina thought and did radiated to the audience, as we watched and shared the experience.

For the teacher

Within each chapter, there are teacher-led, group, paired and individual student exercises. There are extension tasks for the student to practise at home and then show to the class. There are teacher notes and student notes, performance, rehearsal and exam tips for the student. Many of the exercises are student driven, designed for students to work through straight from the book, leaving you free to guide, observe and assess your students at work. At the start of each chapter, there are definitions of the area of the system to be examined. The book is designed so you can lead the initial exercise, and for the student to work through the follow-on exercises in class or at home. Students then have a full record of work on which to evaluate their progress – which is useful to support the BTEC National Performing Arts qualification and for students constructing their International Baccalaureate journals.

After each exercise, it is recommended to evaluate how the exercise went and what the student learned from the exercise. I often encourage students to reflect on the exercise at home, to start the process of gaining solid reference points for truthful acting. In each chapter, there is a range of exercises, so as you work through the system you can choose from a variety of exercises. The book is designed so you can dip in and dip out or use it as an extended programme of study. So, whether you have a week, a month or a half term, you will be able to give your students a broad experience of Stanislavski.

For many, Stanislavski's system is intrinsically linked to naturalism and therefore is to be done with the likes of Ibsen, Strindberg or Chekhov. For me, Stanislavski's system offers the way into any text. In the words of Katie Mitchell, National Theatre director, 'You can use Stanislavsky's techniques regardless of the style or genre of the play or project you are working on.'[2]

With experiencing being at the heart of the system, teachers and students can use it to create the most experimental piece of theatre. A piece of

xx introduction

devised theatre that uses objectives and actions, built on a free and expressive body that utilizes the power of pranic communication and radiation can lead to truly experiential performance.

AT WHAT LEVEL CAN I USE THIS BOOK?

This book is focussed primarily at AS, A2, International Baccalaureate, BTEC National and GCSE drama courses. Each exercise will carry a suggested level for the exercise, with some being suitable for KS3 and one exercise in each chapter suitable for undergraduate level.

With the AQA syllabus at AS and A2, the exercises can be used to interpret a set play, with students working on an extract from a play, and when exploring a set play from the director's point of view.

For the Edexcel syllabus, this book is designed to help you when exploring a play, rehearsing a monologue or duologue and in the performance of a published play. These exercises can be used when examining a set play from the director's point of view.

For the WJEC syllabus, these exercises can be used when working on a practitioner and with a text; when performing scenes or devising a piece; and when looking at a text in a context, performance history and the challenges of acting. Across the A level syllabi, this book would be useful in structuring a piece of devised or original theatre.

For International Baccalaureate students, whether studying in the United States, Kenya or Thailand, the Stanislavski system plays an integral part in all three units: 'Theatre in the making', 'Theatre in performance' and 'Theatre in the world'. The exercises in this book will help you to compile your journal, give you an understanding of the system and prepare you for performance.

At BTEC, the exercises can be used to look at the historical context of performance and when rehearsing for performance and performing to an audience.

At GCSE, this book can be used for lesson ideas to explore drama and is especially useful for Edexcel's Unit 3, 'Drama Performance', in giving students a focus and direction to their devised and scripted work.

For the student preparing for their LAMDA exams, the exercises in this book can form a base on which to progress up the grades. It will also be useful in responding to the examiners' questions as part of the 'Knowledge' section of the exam.

For university and drama school students, you will find many of these exercises helpful for your 'out of class time' work. The student exercises mirror those used at drama school and will be effective in helping you to practise your craft. Chapter 11, 'The acting exercise programme', can be used by actors at any level to practise their skills and keep them 'audition ready'.

1 Objectives

I always start every workshop off the same way, with the **objective** and the **action**. For those new to Stanislavski or those with some experience, the objective and action form the base on which you can build an understanding of how to use Stanislavski's system. The objective and the action are essential tools in deciding what your character wants and is doing within a circumstance. By imagining what your character wants and by deciding on what to do to achieve it (the action), you are not the actor thinking about what you should be doing on stage, but the character wanting to achieve an objective within a set of **given circumstances**. This first chapter will look at the objective, and Chapter 2, action.

I remember when I first realized, as an actor, how having a clear objective affected the creation of a character. I was in my first year at drama school and rehearsing the part of Bamforth in Willis Hall's *The Long and the Short and the Tall*. We were rehearsing a scene with the director, we had already discussed my objective, and we had talked through the given circumstances, within the **bit** of the play we were looking at. I then went away and imagined I was my character, sitting in a hut in the extreme heat of the Malayan jungle. I imagined how I would achieve my objective of wanting to help the Japanese prisoner of war and the actions I would use for that to happen.

The next day, we were showing that bit of the play to the head of acting when, as my character, I looked over at the Japanese prisoner of war and smiled at him, as if to say, 'don't worry mate, I'll look after you'. After the rehearsal, I thought about this smile and where it had come from. I then realized how the objective worked. If you, as the actor, do the work in rehearsal (by imagining being within your given circumstances with an objective), then by the time you get on stage you will be thinking as the character, with clear actions that come from the character and not from you as the actor. You are then on the road to creating a **truthful** character, free of cliché. So, for me, at that moment, I was no longer a drama student but a soldier in the midst of the Malayan jungle, fighting against the injustices of war. I wasn't thinking, 'how do I play this bit?', but 'how do I help this guy?'

action
What we do, as the character, to fulfil our objective.

bit
A play is divided up into manageable sections or units by the actors and director.

given circumstance
The situation the character is in within a particular bit of the play.

objective
What we, as the character, want to achieve within a given set of circumstances.

truthful
Acting is truthful when, based on a set of given circumstances, you are thinking and doing as the character, imagining actively with a free body and a clearly walked through before-time.

Ultimately, a character's objective gives them a direction. By deciding on the character's objectives in a play, you can map out which way your character is going and feel secure in what you, as the character, want on stage.

1 BUILD A SCENE

Student exercise

> **AIM**
>
> To focus your **imagination** on your objective and to explore the actions to achieve that objective. To build and create a number of characters with different objectives in a series of different given circumstances.

AS, A2, IB, BTEC National, GCSE.

imagination
The ability to treat fictional circumstances as if they were real.

- Sit in a semicircle. On your own, take a few seconds to come up with a character and decide what that character does for a living. This could be anything from a plumber or an astronaut to a housewife. Then decide where your character is (the setting) and what they want. One of you will then enter the space and, as your character, with an objective, start to do what your character would be doing in that setting (Figure 1.1). The space then becomes that setting. The objective comes as 'I want to . . .', as in 'I want to do my best' or 'I want to find out'.
- For the rest of you, watch the one person in the space and try to figure out where they are, who they are and what they are doing. When you think you know, join in. Enter as a character from that setting, with an objective (Figure 1.2). It's important that neither actors nor audience speak, and you focus on using your imagination and achieving your objective (Figure 1.3).
- Here's an example:

> I'm a hairdresser and I'm standing in my salon, I'm 32 and an experienced stylist. The girl who is sitting in the chair has long blonde hair and wants a new style. So I imagine my surroundings – the mirrors, the basins, the girl on reception, customers waiting – and I start to decide on my objective. First of all, I look at all the given circumstances. It's 4 o'clock, and I've been in since 10. I was recommended to the girl whose hair I'm cutting by one of her friends. I want to make sure I do a good job on her hair so she comes back regularly and tells all her friends about me. I give myself the objective 'I want to do the best job of styling her hair'.

Figure 1.1
First one up

Figure 1.2
Joining the scene

I now imagine how I want her hair to ideally look and how I am going to do it and I start cutting. I don't think about the audience, just the girl's hair and how I want it to look. I can also start to imagine the girl going out, seeing her friends, them commenting on her hair, and then me getting more clients!

• As I am imagining cutting her hair, the rest of the group who are watching, decide on your character from the setting, give your character an objective and join in. You could be the girl on reception, a man who has finished work coming in for a trim, someone from British Gas checking the meter or a friend waiting for one of the stylists to finish. Allow the scene to develop and explore your objective and what you do to achieve that objective.

Possible settings and characters:

• beach   sunbather
• supermarket   shelf stacker
• classroom   teacher
• office   office worker

Figure 1.3
The full scene

- train   commuter
- operating theatre   surgeon
- circus   lion tamer
- piano removal   removal worker
- beauty salon   beautician
- garage   mechanic.

Notes for the student

For this exercise, allow the given circumstance (the situation you have put your character in) to feed into your objective. So, if you are a lion tamer and you are training a new lion, you will want to be in control and for the lion to do what you want. Don't think about showing your character to the others, just imagine yourself in the circumstances, have your objective and do what your character is doing. If you can't think of what to do, imagine how you would achieve your objective step by step, and that should help.

Stanislavski realized very early in his life that actors were showing their characters rather than believing and **experiencing** them. One way to stop an actor showing his character was to decide on a clear objective or want for that character. As Stanislavski said, objectives 'guide the actor along the proper path and stop him playacting'.[1]

The Stanislavski system really is quite simple. It is a guide for you as actors to help you create truthful characters. If you follow the system, you will be able to create, develop and experience your character. Stanislavski was an actor and director who created a system to help, not only himself as an actor, but other actors. The system is a set of easily accessible tools to help you to act better and gives you, the student, confidence in being able to achieve your goals.

> **experiencing**
> The state where you leave the actor behind and find the character, with everything you do being the product of your character's thoughts and actions.

Notes for the teacher

After each scene, I discuss with each student their character, their objective, where they came from, how old they were, what they wanted in this scene and what they were going to do later.

This exercise works well to start a lesson and focus a group; I often use it with all ages to focus them on their characters. With an A level group, it can be very useful to get them to explore the depth of a character and create a truthful objective that fits the given circumstances they have created. It also allows the student to explore the actions that fulfil the objective and how these actions, when in line with the given circumstance and objective, seem real and believable. For those lively groups, it is also a good attention exercise and a must for Friday afternoons!

For GCSE and younger students, this exercise helps to build confidence in tackling a wide variety of roles and gives the students the first tool that they can use as actors.

Student follow-on exercise: through the character's eyes

It is a common assumption that all the actor's work is done in the rehearsal rooms, when, in reality, some of the most valuable work is done outside rehearsal. Creating a character and engaging your imagination to create a past and a future for your character are often done at home or while going about your daily life.

I often have students tell me they are so busy with coursework, Duke of Edinburgh and swimming practice that they have hardly any time to work on their character. These exercises are designed with you, the busy student, in mind. They can be done anywhere, i.e. walking home, on the bus, in the park or waiting for a tube. I want you to create five characters, each with different jobs, put them each in a circumstance, give them an objective and imagine achieving that objective as your character.

For example: You are an air traffic controller, it is 5 o'clock in the morning, and you have been working all night. You are watching your screens and tracking three aircraft, two of which are circling, and one is coming into land. Imagine the screens and a coffee next to you, decide on your objective and see what happens. You only need about thirty seconds for this exercise. Then think about what it was like – how did your objective work? Was there an **event** that changed your objective?

You can then do the exercise again, changing your objective. You might start with 'I want my shift over and done with', and then you notice that one of the planes is coming into land too early; you would then orientate to what is happening, and your objective could change to 'I want to find out what that plane is doing'. Allow yourself to see the world through your character's eyes and how you are going to get what your character wants.

Here are five suggested characters:

> **event**
> Something that happens that affects what you are thinking and doing.

- an athlete in the changing room before a race
- a pupil in detention
- an MI5 watcher tailing a suspect
- a judge at a beauty contest
- a priest hearing a confession.

By doing exercises like this, you are building up your ability to have an objective and act in a given circumstances while using your imagination.

Throughout his life, Stanislavski spent ten to twenty minutes each day working on exercises within a set of given circumstances!

Whenever I am rehearsing a role, I will often put myself in a circumstance with an objective and see how my character reacts. You'd be surprised how these moments add up and help you to create a character. It's these moments that allow you, the actor, to experience life through your character's eyes, to see what your character wants and how you are going to achieve it.

Exam tip

It is a reality of being on stage that, at some point, you will be distracted either by someone in the audience coughing, a phone going off, an unexpected movement back stage or a fellow actor forgetting their lines. Any of these things could happen during your live assessments or performance for an examiner. If this does happen, here is what to do. You will be standing on stage, aware that you are now thinking about whatever just happened and not your character. So, the first thing to do is relax, and then ask yourself 'what is my objective?'. This will trigger off your objective and pull you back into the context and given circumstances of the piece. You'll be surprised that the answer will pop up and, with it, the rest of the work you have done on your character. Your character's objectives work as a compass, guiding you through the performance. If you ever get lost, you only need to refer to your compass and you will be back on track again.

2 TAXI

AS, A2, IB, BTEC National.

Student exercise

AIM

To have an objective within a set of given circumstances.

Use four chairs to represent a cab and start the improvisations with the driver already sitting in the front of the cab.

- Student A, you are a taxi driver, it is midday, and you've been working since 7 o'clock this morning. You are waiting outside Liverpool Street station. You generally ask a few questions of people in your cab, to get a conversation going; it usually helps to pass the time. Your objective is 'I want to belong'.

- Student B, you will choose a given circumstance and an objective from Table 1.1, hail the taxi and get in. Use the given circumstances to feed into your objective and imagine how you are going to achieve your objective. You will do this exercise three times, each with a different given circumstance and objective, so that you can start to see how having a different objective affects the outcome of the improvisation.

Table 1.1 Taxi scenarios

You have arrived at Liverpool Street Station and are due to meet some old school friends; you are now in your first year at university. You only have the name of the pub you are meeting them in and the street name. You're looking forward to lunch, a couple of drinks and catching up. You hail a cab, jump in and start chatting about your journey. Your objective is 'I want to belong'.

Your train was delayed and you are already five minutes late for your job interview. This is your first interview since leaving university, and you have been getting more and more worked up on the train. You had planned to take a bus to the interview but now decide to hail a cab. You are now really nervous and stressed and need to calm down. Your objective is 'I want to calm myself down'.

You are an American businessman and have arrived at Liverpool Street Station; you have to get to the Gherkin for a meeting and you were told to get off here. You are not really sure where you are and so have decided to get a taxi. This is your first time in London. Your objective is 'I want to orientate'.

You are currently in your AS year and have come down from Birmingham to see your auntie for a couple of days; she told you to get a cab from the station. On the journey down, your boyfriend sent a text saying he needed some 'space'. You tried calling him, but he didn't answer. Your objective is 'I want to be cared for'.

You want to be a singer; you left school last year after A levels to concentrate on singing. You have just auditioned for *The X Factor*, and Simon Cowell said you were 'special'. You have phoned everyone you know and now are desperate to tell the cab driver all about today. Your objective is 'I want to share my good fortune'.

Notes for the student

After each improvisation, think about how having an objective changed the scene. Did it direct you through the scene? Did it help to answer any questions you had? By giving your character an objective, you decide on the path to take within the circumstances you are in. It means that you have something to achieve, something to aim for, and it will drive you through the scene. By having an objective, you can start to see things as your character, within a circumstance, and not as the actor.

Notes for the teacher

The purpose of this exercise is to introduce students to Stanislavski in a practical way. It leaves students with the clear impression of one of the two elements that lie at the heart of the Stanislavski system. When they think about Stanislavski, they think about deciding on what they want as the character, which will lead to what they are going to do to achieve it (the action). By doing this exercise, students start to think, 'what is my character wanting within a set of circumstances', and not, 'what can I do to show my character to the audience'. This is the first step to being active as their character on stage.

Exam tip

For your devised or scripted performances to the examiner, decide on what your objective is during every bit of the play. This will mean you know what direction your character is going in, and therefore the examiner will too. Examiners often comment that a character wasn't really allowed to develop. By carefully structuring the objectives your character has, throughout your piece, you will ensure the development of your character and a happy examiner! For students taking LAMDA exams, one of the set questions asked of you by the examiner will be, 'What is your objective?'. So, a good working knowledge of objectives will be very useful to you. On the day of the exam, go over what your objectives are and the actions you take to achieve them, then go for it and enjoy it.

3 DIVIDING THE TEXT INTO BITS

AS A2, IB, BTEC National, GCSE.

Student exercise

AIM

To understand how to divide the play into bits and use this as a springboard for deciding the character's objective.

Being faced with a whole play or a large section of a play to rehearse can often be a daunting task. So, to make it more manageable, we divide the play up into 'bits'. When dividing up the play into bits, there are three main things to look out for to help us decide when to change bits or how to recognize a new bit:

- when an event happens, whether physical or psychological, that affects what the characters are thinking or doing on stage;
- when a character changes objective and starts wanting something else;
- when a character enters or exits the stage.

Remember that it is the actor and director working together who decide where each bit starts and finishes; it is part of the process of understanding the play and analysing the character's objectives and actions.

In groups, look at the play you are currently working on or look at the last play you read. Alternatively, you can do this exercise with one of the extracts in the exercises in Chapter 5 – either Relationships or Relationships 2.

- Look at the first three pages of your play. Using the three rules for when a bit changes, start to work out where each bit starts and finishes. It's a good idea to number or label each bit, so that everyone knows which bit you are working on. Mark in pencil where the bit starts and finishes. When deciding the name for each bit, you can choose a name that sums up the main event in that bit or what the main thing is that is happening to the characters.
- By working out where each bit starts and finishes, you have taken the first step to finding the objective, which is our next exercise.

Notes for the student

This exercise is great for getting you thinking about the characters and the given circumstances for a particular bit of a play. It will bring up countless questions that, when debated and answered, start to form your core knowledge of the play.

During one workshop on Ibsen's *Hedda Gabler*, we were working out the bits for the section of the play, when one girl, who was to play Hedda, said, 'the more I look at Hedda the more I realise just how complicated she really is. What does she really want?'. This brought about a discussion on how the **super objective** (Chapter 6) can be used and how the character's past is important (Chapter 3). Try to remember the impression of the character from these discussions; you will be able to use this knowledge later as you work through the following chapters in this book.

Student follow-on exercise: naming a bit

Take home the play you are working on and work out the bits for Act 1. Give a name to each bit that sums up for you what is really happening in

super objective
The theme of the play, the sum of all the objectives of the characters; it's what the play is really about. For a character, the super objective is what they want over the course of the play.

the scene. Think about why you changed bits at a given point – was it a change in what the characters were thinking about, or was it an event that had occurred?

Exam tip

For AS students who are rehearsing a monologue or duologue to show a visiting examiner, it's a good idea to divide your piece into bits and then give clear objectives that show the development of your character. It is quite easy to end up with the same train of thought throughout the monologue, so, by dividing the piece into bits, you will identify any psychological or physical events that will affect your character. Allow these events to act as a springboard for the changing objective that releases your actions, creating the depth within the piece. For GCSE students rehearsing a scripted piece, dividing your script into bits will give you a structure you can then build on to create atmosphere; make sure you can pin down when things happen and how they affect your character.

4 FINDING THE OBJECTIVE

AS, A2, IB, BTEC National, GCSE.

Student exercise

AIM

To understand how to find the objective using the given circumstances and taking your first step to harnessing the creative powers of the **subconscious**.

Stanislavski said, 'We must remember the basic principle of our school of acting: the subconscious through the conscious.'[2]

Stanislavski wanted us to delve deep into our characters to explore and tap into their subconscious desires. We can start doing this by first finding the conscious objectives, which will then lead us to the subconscious objectives. When working with objectives, I always start with the conscious objectives and work deeper. It is this process that helps to unlock the subtext and create relationships on stage.

- Select a character from the list in Table 1.2 and, in a group, decide the given circumstances of the character, include their daily life, age, profession, where they live, marital status and hobbies.

relationships
The thoughts we have about others.

subconscious
The part of the mind that influences our thoughts and actions without our being aware of it.

Table 1.2
Finding the objective:
characters

1 A painter and
   decorator who has
   just spilt a can of
   paint on the carpet

2 A university student
   who has just found
   out the girl he has
   liked for ages is now
   going out with his
   best friend

3 A doctor who has to
   deliver bad news to a
   patient

4 A teacher who's just
   given a detention to a
   student who is
   always in trouble

5 A traffic warden
   giving a ticket to an
   OAP driver

- Then, as a group, discuss where exactly they are and what has just happened to them. Once you have gathered all this information, start to decide on an objective: start with a conscious one and then slowly work towards a more subconscious objective. Before you start, look at the example based on character 2 in Table 1.2 to give you an idea of the process and how much detail you need to go into.

The following example is based on character 2.

A university student, Lawrence, is 20 and in his second year studying psychology at Manchester University; it is now April, so he's preparing for the end of year exams. He has been friends with Trish for around six weeks and recently has really started to fancy her. Lawrence has just walked into the refectory after a seminar and sat down with a group of friends. Pete, his best friend, comes up, and the others start asking him what happened between him and Trish last night. Pete smiles, saying he and Trish are now an item.

For Lawrence, his objective would change when he hears Trish's name and the news that she and Pete are now going out. He would have a moment of orientation; then his conscious objective could change to 'I want to change the subject'. His subconscious objective could be 'I want Pete to suffer'. Within the circumstance, Lawrence could feel betrayed and want revenge. By tapping into the subconscious, the **relationship** takes on a new depth; in contrast with the conscious objective 'I want to change the subject', we would miss a lot of the subtext of the situation. There may be any number of alternatives, depending on the given circumstances, which can be explored by you, the student.

- In groups, now give feedback on the scenario you have chosen, outlining your given circumstance, and tell the rest of the group your decisions for the conscious objective and then the subconscious objective.
- As a group, discuss possible alternative subconscious objectives that could work well in the circumstances.
- Look at the other characters in the scene you have created, decide on their objectives, get on your feet and improvise the scene and see what happens.
- Evaluate the improvisation, deciding if the objectives you chose worked within the circumstances, and evaluate how effective your journey into the subconscious has been.

Notes for the teacher

I often use this exercise to help students to put themselves in the shoes of the character and see things through their character's eyes. This exercise works well with all levels and is a vital step to analysing a play. You can use this process with the text you are working on by giving the students the task below and then holding a feedback session and discussion. Encourage the students to sit in a group with their text and a pencil, jotting down for each bit what the objective is and some details on the given circumstances. It's a good idea if students have each page of their text blown up and put into a folder, so they have plenty of room to make notes and write in their character's objectives.

Students may come up with conscious objectives that, through discussion, can be analysed to create a more subconscious objective. If the discussion dries up, follow Stanislavski's lead and get the students on their feet improvising within the circumstances leading up to a changing bit and see where the improvisation takes them. Often, just by being within the circumstance and walking through the actions of the character, the student will discover the objective, organically and truthfully.

Student follow-on exercise: conscious to the subconcious

Now you can turn your new skills to the section of the play you used in the 'Dividing the text into bits' exercise above. You have the bits and so know where the objectives start and end. Choose a character and then work out three conscious objectives and then your three subconscious objectives for the three bits. The best way to come up with the objective is by putting yourself into the character's given circumstances and asking 'what does my character want?'. At this point, you can use the **magic if**. If I was this character within these circumstances, what would I want? In Table 1.3, there are examples of objectives for you to use as a guide.

If you are stuck, come up with a starter objective and then go into class and discuss your findings with your teacher and fellow students. It is amazing how talking through the given circumstance with others can trigger off an idea that you would never have come up with on your own.

> **magic if**
> The question, 'what if', that the actor asks themselves to trigger the imagination within a given set of circumstances.

Table 1.3 Objectives list

I want to do my best	I want to lose myself	I want to be remembered	I want to enjoy my time
I want to be the winner	I want to be important	I want to be envied	
I want to find out	I want to provoke anger	I want to be rich	I want to succeed
I want to orientate		I want to be poor	I want to understand
I want to suffer	I want to be the centre of attention	I want to have no responsibilities	I want to be rejected
I want to be superior			I want to please
I want to be special	I want to do my duty	I want to be famous	I want to despair
I want to belong	I want to impress	I want to be strong	I want to be frustrated
I want to be cared for	I want to be admired	I want to have peace of mind	
I want to be liked	I want to be powerful		I want to be accepted

Rehearsal tip

During his early years, Stanislavski and his actors spent a substantial part of the rehearsal process sitting around a table analysing the play and the characters. Later on in his life, Stanislavski favoured getting the actors up on their feet sooner, so that they, as actors, didn't lose inspiration for their role.

I would recommend, when working on a text in groups, especially at A level, BTEC and IB, that you don't get too bogged down in the analysis stage. Make informed decisions after you have done your research, decide on your objectives within a bit, then get on your feet and give it a go (Figure 1.4)! Have a look at the '**Active Analysis**' exercise in Chapter 9 to help you.

Figure 1.4
Students with the objective 'I want to be the winner'. Constance on the left and Amber on the right both have the objective 'I want to be the winner'. You can see how they are both mentally and physically engaged in achieving that objective. When you look into their eyes, you can see they are thinking about what they are going to do next, and, when you look at their bodies, you get an impression of how they will move to achieve their objective

AS, A2, IB, BTEC National, undergraduate.

5 ACTION WITHOUT OBJECTS

Student exercise

AIM

For you to test the skills you have learned and to start the process of building and creating a character.

Stanislavski believed that actors, like singers, dancers or gymnasts, must be in training every day. An actor cannot turn up at the theatre and expect to create a truthful performance if he has not prepared himself and has not regularly been working on his skills.

This exercise gives you the chance to create, explore, rehearse and experience, building on the skills learned in this chapter.

* I want you to think of an everyday activity, for example, washing up, making a cup of tea, shaving or putting on make-up (Figure 1.5). At home, rehearse your chosen activity three times with the objects needed and three times without the objects needed (Figure 1.6) Decide on the given circumstances and objective when performing your activity. For example: If my activity is washing up, I'll go into my kitchen and wash a plate and knife and fork three times. I give myself an objective from the given circumstances – so, if it's the morning and

> **Active Analysis**
> A rehearsal technique where actors analyse a bit of the play 'on their feet'. The actors decide on the main event, an action for each character, and then improvise that bit.

Figure 1.5
Washing up with objects

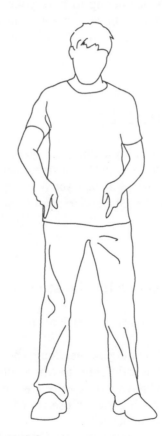

Figure 1.6
Washing up without objects

I'm quickly washing my breakfast things before work, I may have the objective 'I want to have it over and done with'. Alternatively, it may be the evening, and I've got ten minutes to kill before the news starts, so I decide I might as well wash up, and my objective then could be 'I want to bide my time'.

- Observe your surroundings and the objects you have in your hands – what the objects feel like, their size and weight. With the washing up example, I would need to imagine what the water felt like on my hands and the temperature of the water.
- Decide on what you have been doing so far that day and what you are going to be doing later. If it was morning, I would imagine that I have just woken up, and, for evening, I would imagine all the events that had occurred that day.
- I then imagine washing up in a different room, not the kitchen, without the objects, using the objective and my imagination to guide me. So you need to go and stand in a different room and practise the exercise, remembering to have your objective and imagine your surroundings and the objects in your hands.
- You will then come into class and show your classmates and see what they think.

Student performance tip

The key to this exercise is preparation; if you rush your rehearsals, the end product will look rushed. Take your time; allow your imagination time to build your surroundings and the weight of the objects. Use your objective to guide you and don't panic if you think you've lost your objective, just relax and slowly imagine what you wanted to achieve. Remember, Stanislavski never wanted you to force anything – so relax, try your best and enjoy it.

Questions for the student

Here is a list of questions to ask yourself after the exercise:

- How did you feel doing the exercise in front of the audience?
- Was it different to when you were rehearsing at home? If so, why?
- What was your objective, and how did you decide on your objective?
- Was it easier to use your imagination at home rather than in front of an audience?
- If you were going to prepare for this task again, would you do anything differently? If so what?

Notes for the teacher

With many students, the exercise can become hurried, and they lose the imagined objects and the objective as their attention moves from the 'action without objects' to the audience. If this happens, allow them to do the exercise again, focussing their attention on the physical actions and the objective. Reassure the student that, when you look at free body (Chapter 4), they will be given tools to move their attention from the audience and on to their actions. This exercise lets the student experience having an objective that manifests in action to achieve what their character wants. Students will start to see that the actions they perform to achieve their objective are not just physical. This leads onto the next chapter, where we will examine action in greater detail. Now would be a good time to introduce the idea, 'in every physical action there's something psychological, and there is something physical in every psychological action'.[3] The students can then have this in the back of their mind in preparation for looking at actions.

I use this exercises early on with students to get them up on their feet and experiencing. Often, they make a breakthrough and will see how, from imagining their objective and the given circumstances, they start to perform an action, and that action was truthful because it had a purpose behind it. One student, who was making tea as her 'action without object', was halfway through the exercise when she looked up and seemed to look into the distance. Afterwards, I asked why she looked up, and at first she couldn't remember doing so but, as we talked through the exercise, she said that she had started thinking about sitting in the lounge and drinking the tea while watching TV. Her looking up was a truthful action that came from her objective and so felt real to the audience. For the student, she realized that putting herself within a circumstance and deciding what she wanted led her to using actions to achieve it. This was a breakthrough moment for her that she could then take on to use with text work and performances.

Student follow-on exercise: logic and sequence

* Look at the following quote from Stanislavski:

  You must first think about, then carry out the action. In this way, thanks to the logic and sequence of what you do, you approach truth by a natural path and from truth you go to belief and thence to genuine experiencing.[4]

* Using the knowledge you have gained from this exercise, what do you think Stanislavski meant?
* Having just experienced how the thought leads to action, did you feel your acting becoming more truthful?

Student follow-on exercise 2: action without objects for the character

You can use the 'Action without objects' exercise with a variety of characters to practise having an objective and at the same time develop your imagination.

- Choose a character and physical action from the list below. Imagine the given circumstances of the character and what their objective is. Imagine the surroundings and the objects around you and the ones in hand. Think about what you have done so far today and what you will do later.
- Rehearse the action without objects and then evaluate how it went. As an actor, you will often have to self-evaluate your performance to see where you can improve for the future.

This exercise will help you to create and build a character using the objective, the given circumstances and actions.

Character	Physical action
Soldier	Firing on the rifle range
Traffic warden	Giving a ticket
Masseuse	Giving a massage
Electrician	Wiring a house
Chess grand master	Playing chess
Gardener	Planting a tree
Pilot	Taking off
Librarian	Sorting books
Nurse	Giving an injection

AS, A2, IB, BTEC National.

6 THE OBJECTIVE IN LIFE

Teacher led extension exercise

AIM

To see how the objective works in life so you can transfer this knowledge to the stage.

This exercise is quick and easy, but invaluable as an example of how the objective works.

- During a discussion or after a previous exercise, ask a student to go and open the door. Just before the student reaches the door, ask him or her to sit down again. Then ask them to tell you what they thought and did from the moment you asked them to open the door. Ask the student to recall exactly what they thought and saw in their mind's eye.

On one occasion with this exercise, one student said that she imagined opening the door and heard the 'whoosh' sound the door made. Often, students will say they saw the door handle in their mind's eye before getting up. One student said her first thought was to lean forward and to push herself off the chair. Students will often say they had a clear impression of the path they were going to take physically. This exercise shows that, in life, we have a series of objectives – in this case, 'I want to open the door', and they come with pictures of how we achieve this objective and an impression of the actions we will perform.

- Ask the next student to open the window and follow the same process. I use this exercise to show how, in life, a small action comes with the use of the five senses and is perfectly mapped out for us to achieve this object-ive. Therefore, on stage, our objectives need to have the same qualities – they need to be real and draw on what we hear, see, taste, smell and feel.

Notes for the teacher

I use this exercise to allow the student to have a reference point for an objective in life to then compare with the objective on stage. I remind them that, on stage, we often have longer objectives than the ones in this exercise, but that the qualities that we experienced in this exercise, which make up the objective, are always present. I find this exercise helps students think about the process of acting and how we recreate what happens in life on stage.

Student follow-on exercise: self-observation

Over the course of the next twenty-four hours, observe how you carry out simple tasks that you normally do without thinking, for example, going to the bus stop or opening the fridge door. Recall the qualities of the objective and the part the senses played in imagining your objective. Use this informa-tion to see how the objective works for you. After an event has occurred, look back and see what effect the circumstances had on your objective.

OBJECTIVES

The objective is a want. It is what we as the character want to achieve within a given set of circumstances.

The objective is what the character wants through each bit of the play. It is both psychological and physical, an impression of what we can achieve in the situation we are in. With an objective comes an impression, both physical and mental, of the obstacles we have to overcome to achieve our objective.

The objective comes from the character's given circumstances. The objective comes as 'I want to . . .', as in 'I want to do my best'.

The given circumstance is the situation the character is in within a particular bit of the play.

The subconscious is the part of the mind that influences our thoughts and actions without us being aware of it.

2 Action

In the first chapter, we worked on the objective (our 'want') and now we will look at the action (what we 'do'). The objective and action run in tandem, for, when we want something, we immediately start to imagine what we will do to achieve it. The objective leads to the action.

It is the action that helps drive us through the bit of the text to achieve what we, as the character, want.

We have an inner action and an outer action. Our inner action is what we really are doing to achieve our want, and the outer action is what we want people to see we are doing and think we are doing. The outer action works like a cover for the inner action.

For example: a hotel reception worker who has just split up from her partner and has an eight-hour shift ahead of her may have, as an outer action, 'I do my duty', while their inner action may be 'I pity myself'. If I was booking into the hotel, I might get an impression that something was wrong with the receptionist. I would be picking up on her inner action. The same happens on stage: a character has an outer action, which as the audience we immediately pick up on, but as we watch we start to get an impression of something else going on – that is the inner action working. This chapter will explore how to use actions through a variety of exercises. All the exercises are student exercises, with the last exercise being a teacher-led extension exercise.

The action comes as an active verb, such as I belong, I enjoy, I reject, I take pride, I challenge, I suffer.

On stage, our actions are always grounded in the given circumstances of the character. The question we always ask ourselves as actors is: What does our character do within a set of given circumstances?

For you, the action will become a key tool, both in the analysis of text and in its performance.

7 THE PSYCHOPHYSICAL ACTION

AS, A2, IB, BTEC National, undergraduate.

Student exercise

psychophysical
The combination of what we are thinking and doing that works across the system. What we think and do working together in harmony.

AIM

To experience the **psychophysical** nature of actions. To understand how the action is a combination of what we do, both mentally and physically.

- From Table 2.1, choose an action, and then go in front of the class, put yourself in the given circumstance and 'do' your action.

Table 2.1 Action and given circumstance

I share	cutting the piece of cake
I attack	punching an assailant who is about to attack you
I brush off	brushing off a fly buzzing around you
I warm up	warming up before going on to dance
I reject	closing the door in someone's face
I belong	(to be done in pairs, with you greeting each other)
I orientate	looking at a map trying to work out the direction to go in
I force myself	drinking foul-tasting medicine
I invite	answering the door to invite a friend in
I demand	someone owes you money
I shrug off	someone tries to hold you

- The first example is 'I share'. Imagine you are standing before a piece of cake and have to share it between you and someone else (Figure 2.1). You want to make sure that you both have equal slices. You have the knife in your hand and you cut the cake. Start to build up the given circumstances and allow them to feed into the action.
- If your action is 'I attack', imagine someone is about to attack you. If you don't hit them first, you will be in real trouble (Figure 2.2). Your punch has to knock them off their feet to give you a chance to get away.
- The rest of the class who are watching now comment using the following criteria:
  - Did they have the action they were meant to have?
  - Did the action seem believable?

Figure 2.1
I share

Figure 2.2
I attack

- Did it seem to you, as the audience, that the actor's mind and body were combined in the action?
- Did the pieces look as if they were of equal size/Do you think the punch would have knocked the other person to the ground?

Notes for the student

After each action, think about how much of the action was physical and how much was psychological. Remember to create the circumstances and allow the action to come from them. Don't force the action; allow it to be a combination of what you are thinking and doing. If there is an action you are unfamiliar with, create a circumstance in which you would have that action and say the action silently in your mind. This will help to trigger off an impression of the action, which you can then use within the exercise.

Notes for the teacher

I suggest using this exercise with students at AS and A2, IB and BTEC. The main purpose of this exercise is for the student to start to see how the psychological and physical work hand in hand, and it allows the class to start building reference points for having an action on stage.

When I work with students looking at actions, I always find it works best to get them up on their feet, give them a range of actions, let them start to find out what the different actions are like and then evaluate the whole process. It puts the emphasis on the student exploring and experiencing, which fits with Stanislavski's vision of the system being a set of practical tools for the actor to discover and enhance the skills they have.

For you, the teacher, the end goal would be that, during a rehearsal with an AS student preparing their monologue or a student rehearsing for a BTEC performance, you could say to the student, 'why don't you try the action "I belong"', and the student takes that on board and can use it within the circumstances. For the boys in the class, the 'I attack' often becomes a chance to knock the assailant into the next room. The results are often highly believable, and, as I often say to the boys, being able to throw a credible stage punch is quite an asset!

Teacher extension task: actions in the world

Give the students this quote from Stanislavski – 'Stage action must be inwardly well-founded, in proper, logical sequence and possible in the real world'[1] – and ask them to relate this to the exercise they have just done; ask if they thought they were starting to achieve actions that are 'possible in the real world'. This task will help students to see that actions are not for the audience but to be within a context.

Student individual exercise: labelling actions

Often, we can look at how things are in life to guide us on stage; this is true of actions. Observe the actions people have and try to give a label to them. For example, the other day I was in Tesco, and the woman in front of me caught her shin on the edge of a box; she turned around and said 'stupid box' and kicked it. Her action was 'I tell off', and the psychological and physical were combined perfectly, working together. Shock, pain, anger, frustration and embarrassment all combined in that kick. It made me smile at how we use actions in all kinds of ways and how the pain for the lady caused an involuntary action that almost defied logic.

Start to watch for people doing the same thing, but with very different actions born out of different circumstances. A mum pushing a buggy along the street may have time to kill and is walking slowly, with the action 'I bide my time', or another mum belting down the street, late to pick up her older child from school, has the action 'I panic'.

Performance tip

Many top directors use actions during their rehearsal process. For you, when directing other students or acting in a group, the ability to label what you want someone to do makes working together much easier. On your script, jot down the action that goes with a line or a bit of the text, to help remind you when going over the scene again. Keep a pencil with you throughout rehearsals, so you don't forget anything.

8 WHAT'S MY ACTION?

AS, A2, IB, BTEC National, GCSE.

Student exercise

AIM

To start using different actions in different circumstances and to focus your action within the scene.

- Sit in a semicircle, with an empty chair in front of you with a book on it. One student leaves the room and decides on an action from the list in Table 2.2, or is given an action by the teacher.
- The student then enters the room, picks up the book and starts reading – all with the action they have decided on.
- For the student entering, imagine a circumstance in which you would read with your chosen action. The action may mean that you don't actually get much reading done; for example, you could be waiting for a train and you see a pretty girl sitting on a bench and you go and sit opposite her (Figure 2.3). The action you have chosen could have been 'I impress' or 'I provoke interest'.
- Or, you could be in the library and you've just been told to stop talking – so you go back to your chair and start reading (Figure 2.4). Your action could be 'I sulk', 'I lose myself from embarrassment' or 'I cringe'.

- Give yourself time to prepare outside the room, when you have decided on your action and the circumstances, enter with that action and see what happens. Try not to think about the audience; instead, imagine the circumstances you are in and the action.
- As a group, decide on what action the person reading had. Don't shout it out, but go around the class one by one, saying what the action is. Work out what the majority decision is and then ask the person reading if it's right.
- To start with, you may all be a bit off when guessing the action, but, as you practise this exercise, you'll get better and better at spotting actions. Combined with your observation work from 'The psychophysical action' exercise above, you'll be identifying actions before you know it.
- For the student reading with the action, think back over the exercise. Do you think you had the action you had originally chosen, or did you have your own actor's action? You may have started with the decided action but then switched actions as you start to think about your audience.
- For those observing, look at the list of actions in Table 2.2 while you are watching the student read and see which fits the best. This list is not exhaustive, but a sample of actions.

Table 2.2 Actions list

I enjoy	I brush off	I long for	I lose myself
I look forward	I despair	I condescend	I blame
I orientate	I find a reason	I get a grip on myself	I suffer
I belong	I humble myself	I despair	I provoke irritation
I provoke interest	I impress	I flirt	I punish
I take pride	I find out	I relax	I put down
I cajole	I denigrate	I bide my time	I envy
I cover up	I do my duty	I tease	I reflect
I force myself	I tempt	I provoke anger	I regret
I remember	I rehearse	I needle	I tell off
I scream for help	I shrink	I search for clues	I plot
I wait	I fascinate	I demand obedience	I panic
I tease	I divulge	I insult	I protest
I revel	I observe	I assess	I challenge
I stand my ground	I dread	I pass my time	I question
I work myself up	I do my best	I let go	I gorge myself
I lure	I reject	I cringe	I sulk
I taunt	I provoke fear	I dream	I brace myself
I sneer	I gloat	I entice	I postpone
I coax	I seduce	I pity myself	

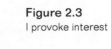

Figure 2.3
I provoke interest

Figure 2.4
I sulk

Extending the exercise: the action and the circumstance

• You can now extend the exercise in a whole range of circumstances, not using the book as a prop.

  • You leave the room, then come back in with an action and allow the action and the given circumstances to determine what you do. For example, outside the room I decide my action is 'I gloat'. I come in and imagine I've just won in a card game against someone I've always disliked and they are sitting in front of me quietly fuming. Using the action as your guide, you can add improvised dialogue to create a small scene.
  • The rest of the class guesses the action, as before.
  • You can start slowly adding other areas of the system you've learned. Ask yourself, what is my objective? Within these circumstances I've created, what would my objective be?

Student follow-on exercise: actions and the role

• At home, walk through one of the two scenarios with the given actions. Rehearse it a number of times, until the actions flow into each other as the events happen. Afterwards, think about the physical and mental changes you went through as the character.

  • Imagine you are a junior doctor on your rounds with a senior doctor, he has just been paged, and you are waiting for his return; your action is 'I bide my time'. A nurse from the next ward shouts to you to come quickly; your action becomes 'I orientate'. The nurse has pressed the alarm button; a baby in the incubation unit is severely distressed and is breathing highly erratically. Your action stays as 'I orientate' but is now directed to the baby's condition. You can't see what the problem is, and your action becomes 'I panic'. You decide the oxygen delivery machine must be faulty, and the nurse quickly changes it; your action is 'I keep my fingers crossed'. The baby starts to calm, as the senior doctor races up and evaluates the situation; he looks over, smiles and winks at you. You're action becomes 'I take pride'.
  • Imagine you are a soldier and have been in Afghanistan for two weeks and have just been put on guard. It's midnight, and your action is 'I do my duty'. You hear a shot and see a flash in the distance, and your action becomes 'I orientate'. After ten seconds, you hear a voice pleading from the darkness, and your action becomes 'I panic'. You then hear an officer come up behind you and say 'Don't worry son, I'll deal with this'. Your action then becomes 'I thank'.
  • You can then come into class and show the others your work.

Audition tip

For those of you thinking of auditioning for drama schools and university courses, an understanding of how to use actions will come in very useful. As part of the audition process for drama school, you may be asked to take part in workshops where you have to improvise around various circumstances. Drama schools are often looking for students who can play a range of characters and are emotionally flexible. The ability to use actions means you can change emotional states quickly, as required within the circumstances. If it's a quick improvisation, you can say to yourself, I'll have the action 'I tell off' to start, and when the event occurs I'll then go into 'I suffer'.

Performance tip

Remember, as actors we don't 'show' an emotion; instead, we have an action from a set of given circumstances that will help to create that emotion. So don't try to act 'anger'; decide on the action that will create 'anger' and have that action within a given set of circumstances.

Notes for the teacher

With this exercise, some students will slip into 'showing the action' to the audience; remind them that, on stage, you are not showing the action to an audience but experiencing an action from an imagined set of circumstances. It may be a good idea to talk through the first one using one of my examples. After a few students have gone up, they should start to get used to spotting the action and will start to see how changing the action can have a real effect on the scene. Students have a lot of fun with this, and it can also be used effectively as a warm-up exercise, to start the lesson by getting students thinking and doing on their feet.

9 THE TRAFFIC WARDEN

Student exercise

AS, A2, IB,
BTEC National,
GCSE.

AIM

To practise having an action within a set of given circumstances.

Figure 2.5
Students practising actions. Constance, on the left, while rehearsing a bit from *The Seagull* (see the exercise on Relationships in Chapter 5) with the actions 'I long for' and 'I suffer'; Amber, on the right, practising the action 'I demand', where she put herself within an imagined circumstance and let the action guide her. You can see the demanding both in her eyes and the physical movement

Two-person improvisation

- You are a traffic warden, it's the last day of the month and you have given ninety-eight tickets so far this month. If you give a hundred by the end of the day, you will get a bonus this month. You have been skulking around the high street all day waiting for someone to park illegally. A car pulls up, and a young woman rushes into Boots; you should give her a few minutes but walk straight over to the car and tap her registration plate into your handheld machine. 'Ninety-nine', you think, only one more to go for the bonus. The mum rushes out carrying a small bag and she starts to have a go at you. This is where the improvisation will start. Your action is 'I provoke anger'. This means, within the circumstances, you want to wind her up, knowing that she's already got the ticket and you can't take it back because it's already gone through on the machine. These little disagreements keep you entertained throughout the day. Everything you think, say and do is with the action 'I provoke anger'.

- You are a young mum; you have a baby daughter who is eleven months old; at around lunchtime today, she started to get a temperature, so you gave her the last of the Calpol. You are worried that the effects of the Calpol will soon wear off and you need to get some more. You leave a message with your husband to pick up some Calpol on his way home. He arrives back home never having got the message. You grab the car keys and drive to Boots; you see a space with parking restrictions but decide that getting the Calpol before the shop shuts is more important, and anyway you'll only be a couple of minutes. You come out the shop and see the traffic warden; you are enraged – it's only been one minute. Your action is 'I tell off'. Everything you think, say and do is with the action 'I tell off'.

- Start the improvisation at the point the traffic warden and the young mum meet. Give it a go and see what happens.
- As the audience, did you feel that the actors had the actions they were asked to have? If not, what action do you think they had? Did the action seem to be truthful, a blend of the psychological and physical?

Notes for the student

For the first two students up, you will have to orientate to what it is like improvising with an action; however, by the time the group has done a couple of improvisations, you will understand fully and wonder how you ever used to improvise without deciding on the action beforehand.

Students will often say to me that having an action in their improvisations means they know exactly what to do, and that it gives them a focus and a way into their character. The next couple of exercises will be action improvisations for you to practise as a group. One thing to remember: if you commit 100 per cent to the improvisation and the action and really give it a go, you'll enjoy it more, and so will the audience.

Student follow-on exercise: shopping

This is one of my favourite individual exercises and one that gets results. I choose a couple of actions and then go into a shop and buy a newspaper or a pint of milk with the chosen actions. I change actions mid transaction and see if it makes a difference. As an actor, you are putting yourself in a circumstance and practising using different actions and so building up your actor's flexibility. For example: I would walk into the shop with 'I belong' and, as I'm looking for my money, change to 'I pity myself'. Be careful which actions you choose: 'I attack' may not be the best idea!

- So, first look at the list of actions in Table 2.2. Choose a couple and then go and buy a pint of milk. Afterwards, check if you had the action you decided you were going to have. This is excellent preparation for evaluating your performance when you come off stage.

Stanislavski wanted his actors to be working on exercises and improvisations throughout their careers. In the same way a pianist will rehearse a few hours each day, the actor always needs to be working on key skills. These follow-on exercises enable you, the student actor, to stay tuned and performance-ready. Today, I do little exercises as I go around my daily life; often I'll put myself in a situation with an action and see what happens!

Notes for the teacher

When running Stanislavski workshops, I often only have time for one or two exercises on each main element of the system. For actions, these improvisations and the exercise 'Action corners', below, are usually the exercises I choose, primarily because they get students on their feet and acting with an action. I don't usually give an introduction, but just give the students the scenarios and let them have a go. I have yet to meet a group that, after twenty minutes, does not 'get' actions. By getting on their feet and with the others watching, the students can see the action working and they very quickly start to see when a student has the action talked about or when they have an action of their own choosing. By the third improvisation, I change the action mid improvisation, and the students see how this completely changes what is happening and they start to see how they can use actions themselves in the rehearsal process.

AS, A2, IB,
BTEC National,
GCSE.

10 THE AIR STEWARD

Student exercise

Two-person improvisation

- You have just recently got a job with a large American bank and have just had a meeting with your new boss. He wants to send you on a training course to the head office in Washington. You have always had a fear of flying and tell him that you have never flown and won't be able to go. Your boss cracks his college boy grin and said 'You fly out Friday, from Heathrow'. You decide that this may be a good opportunity to come to terms with your fear and start packing. The improvisation will start with you on the plane and taxiing to the runway; you press the crew alert button above your head. Your action is

'I panic', but remember you are a professional businessperson on a crowded plane.

- You are an air steward; you have recently become a senior crew-member, which means you are in charge of two other crewmembers on the flight. You have the middle section of the plane to look after. One of the crewmembers in your charge has just left training school and will need your help; the other went out last night and looks seriously hung over. You want your section to run smoothly so you can check up on the other two. You notice the unsettled passenger in your section and hope they're not going to give you too much grief. The improvisation starts with you responding to the crew alert button above the unsettled passenger. Your action is 'I put them in their place'. To cover this up, you have an outer action, the one you want people to see, of 'I offer help' and, of course, your best smile.

- Improvise the scene and then evaluate as a group using these questions:

  - As the audience, did you feel that the actors had the actions they were asked to have?
  - If not, what action do you think they had?
  - Did the action seem to be truthful? A blend of the psychological and physical?
  - Did the situation seem real to you?

Notes for the teacher

With the action 'I put them in their place', the air steward almost slips in this action by default when faced with a nervous or difficult passenger. After years of dealing with difficult passengers, this action has become a means to achieving a quiet flight and an action they go into almost without realizing. 'Putting them in their place' means it's a lot less trouble for him in the long run.

Some students will just not be able to have the action decided upon and will slip into the actions they use in everyday life. Other students will start by having the action, but then may slip into another action and then back to the original. This shows that they have started to use the action decided upon and they are definitely on the right tracks. I often remind students that, like everything, it just takes practice – the more you practise having an action within a set of given circumstances, the better you will get at it.

When boys play the air steward, they often tend to go for the outrage-ously camp option – which can lead to a sketch-show style improvisation – so I tend to remind the class that not all stewards are camp!

11 THE COWBOY BUILDER

Student exercise

Two-person improvisation

- You are a housewife. Attached to your bedroom you have a walk-in wardrobe that you have always wanted to turn into an en suite bathroom. Your husband said it's too small, but you're determined to get a professional opinion. You Google builders in your local area and give one of them a call; they say they will send one of their builders around. You give them the measurements on the phone and a rough idea of what you want. When the builder arrives, you show him the walk-in wardrobe. Your first action is 'I look forward'. Halfway through the improvisation, you get an impression that this builder may be a bit shifty. Your action then becomes 'I test'. You then become much more interested in the price and the reliability of the builder.
- You are a builder; your boss is more interested in a quick profit than doing a good job. He calls you up and asks you to go and look at a job converting a walk-in wardrobe. He says the measurement are tight, so go in there and enjoy it, tell her she can have whatever she wants, and we'll get a deposit up front, do a day's work and say it can't be done. Your action is 'I enjoy' and, as your boss said give her what she wants, if she wants marble tell her you can do marble. The housewife's action will change about halfway through the improvisation; see how the change in her action effects your action.
- Improvise the scene with the change in action and then evaluate how the change affected the improvisation.
- From the audience's perspective, how did the change of action alter the scene?

12 THE ACTION AND THE TEXT

Student exercise

AIM

To use actions with text.

- Read the extract below from *A Doll's House*.
- Decide on the main action for each character in that bit. You can refer to the list of actions in Table 2.2 to help you.
- As well as a main action for a bit, you can also give actions to an individual line. Decide on an action for the two highlighted lines.
- With a partner, try out the actions by getting up on your feet and improvising the scene. See if your chosen actions fit; if they don't, try another one until you get an action that you think fits the best.

A Doll's House, Henrik Ibsen, Act Two

Nora	Come here, Dr Rank. I want to show you something.
Rank	[*sits*] What is it?
Nora	Look!
Rank	**Silk stockings.**
Nora	Flesh-colored! Aren't they lovely! Of course, it's dark here now, but tomorrow . . . No, no, no you can only look at the feet. Oh well, you might as well see a bit higher up, too.
Rank	Hm . . .
Nora	Why are you looking so critical? Don't you think they'll fit?
Rank	I couldn't possibly offer any informed opinion about that.
Nora	[*looks at him for a moment*] Shame on you. [*hits him lightly across the ear with the stockings*] **Take that!** [*folds them up again*]

A Doll's House, in *Four Major Plays*, Henrik Ibsen,
Oxford World Classics, 2008. By permission
of Oxford University Press.[2]

Notes for the student

Think about finding the inner action and how you can start to bring the subtext alive by choosing inner actions that reflect what the character really is thinking and doing. The actions you choose will help to determine what the audience will understand about the character.

For example, if, for Nora's line 'Take that', you choose the action 'I tell off', you would be choosing an action that reinforces the spoken line. Whereas, if you choose 'I flirt', that would be closer to an inner action, and the audience would start to see the subtext of the scene and Nora's character. Often, what we say and what we are thinking are very different, and it's through actions that you, as the actor, can explore your character's subtext.

If you have a play you are working on at the moment, you can always choose a bit and a line from that play, work out the actions and try them out, in the same way as I have done here.

Years ago, I was doing a play with a director, and we were analysing a scene. I suggested an action for my character, and he said, 'You can't have that, I don't think it's on the list'. I remember at the time thinking, 'there is no list'! The director believed there to be a rigid system for acting, with a right and a wrong answer, rather than an experiential process of collaboration between actor and director. On the contrary: if you actively imagine the circumstance and come up with an action, the chances are you'll be right.

Rehearsal tip

Being able to give a line an action means you never have to think about how a line should be said. Instead, you just ask yourself, 'what is my action for this line?'. Likewise, if you don't know what to 'do' on stage, decide on your action and 'do' that.

Notes for the teacher

Working out actions for text is a valuable tool for the student. Whenever you have a piece of text, the actor can bring it alive using actions. Students working with texts such as Martin Crimp's Attempts on her Life *or Sarah Kane's* 4.48 Psychosis, *which people may not normally associate with using the Stanislavski system, can benefit greatly from the structure that actions can bring to the rehearsal process.*

Using actions comes in very handy when directing the 'annual production'. You can do a couple of these exercises with students and then, during the rehearsal process, use actions as a way of communicating your ideas to your cast. You will probably have limited time, and having a tool that can produce results will help you immensely during the rehearsal process.

AS, A2, IB, BTEC National, undergraduate.

13 ACTION CORNERS

Teacher-led extension exercise

AIM

This exercise is intended to stretch students and should be used as an extension task to further the knowledge and experience of the students. This exercise further examines the role of the inner action and how psychophysical actions work in practice.

- One student is standing in the middle of the room, with another student seated in each of the four corners. The other students and the teacher fill in the gaps. Each of the students in the four corners prepares a simple question to ask the student in the middle (Figure 2.6). For example:

- How old are you?
- What star sign are you?
- Where were you born?
- Do you have any brothers and sisters?

- The teacher nods to one of the students in the corner; they then ask their question (Figure 2.7).
- Before the student answers, the teacher gives the student in the middle an action from the list in Table 2.2, and the student answers with that action (Figure 2.8).

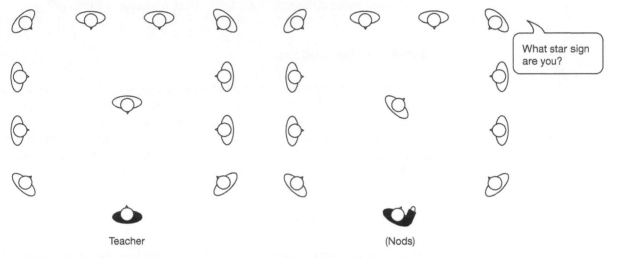

Figure 2.6 Preparing a question

Figure 2.7 Asking a question

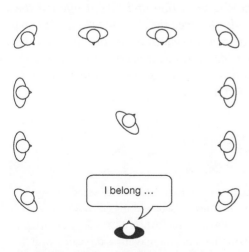

Figure 2.8 Answering with the given action

- The rest of the class observes to see if the student has the action given by the teacher. The teacher then nods to the next student in the corner, they ask a question, and the teacher gives another action and so on.
- To start, do one action at a time and then comment and evaluate. You can then go around four times as the students gain in experience. After each student has had a go, evaluate each set of four actions and decide if the student had the action decided upon. The student can comment on what actions they found it easy to have and what actions they need to practise. Ask students not to think of an outer action but to just have the inner action. Discuss the relationship between the thought and the movement within the action, and what it felt like to have different actions – for example: Did you move differently with 'I tell off' as opposed to 'I belong'?

Notes for the student

As the question comes to you, turn to that person so you can direct the action to them; don't hold back on the actions, give them a full 100 per cent. I recently did this exercise in a college in Leicester, where one of the girls was given 'I tease'. She looked the boy who had asked the question up and down, smiled, her head moved slightly to the side, and she answered. Everything she thought and did came directly from the action, to great effect.

Notes for the teacher

This exercise enables the students to begin to observe how they use actions and to understand the internal and external process of using actions. Allow students to really examine the process of having an action and how it affected them mentally and physically. It's a good idea to video the class and then, in the next lesson, play it back, so that students can see what actions they had and how they worked and looked from the outside. As students get better at this exercise, you can start speeding up, so the student will practise moving quickly from one action to the next, as they would do in a play.

Performance tip

As students of drama and the actors of the future, you have the potential to be cast in any role. Some roles you will slip into and feel right at home with; others will jar, and you'll have difficulty seeing things through the eyes of that character. Examine the actions you can use easily and which ones you have more difficulty with and practise the ones you have difficulty with. For example, if you are quite mild-mannered, you may have problems with 'I tell off', so that's the one you need to practise. If you don't, you can almost guarantee that, in your first audition, the director will say, 'That's very good, this time can you do it angry and really have a go at them'.

While I was training, I was cast to play an older character with a drink problem, who had wasted his life and now regretted it. In the play, there was a young, dashing soldier, which I obviously thought was the better part for me! I struggled with my character and remember having to go away and improvise with the actions of my character to start to understand the character. It took a while, but eventually my actions as the character became clearer, and I could start to use them successfully within the circumstances of the play. Looking back now, I can see why I was cast in that role. It was to challenge me as an actor and make me work outside my comfort zone. I had played a number of roles like the soldier and could have fairly easily slipped into that role, but then I would never have understood what it is to experience a character quite different from myself.

ACTION

An action is what we do as the character to fulfil our objective.

If the objective is the 'want', the action is the 'doing'.

An action is the combination of both the psychological and the physical; as Stanislavski says,

> 'Acting is action – mental and physical.'[3]

We have on stage an outer action and an inner action.

On stage, we do not 'act' an emotion; we have an action within a given circumstance that creates an emotion.

Actions are at the heart of the rehearsal technique Active Analysis that we will study in Chapter 9.

3 Imagination

As Stanislavski said, 'not a single scene, not one single step onstage must be performed mechanically, without an inner reason, that is without the imagination.'[1]

Imagination is the oil of the system; without our imaginations, everything would soon grind to a halt. You as students will use your imagination at every stage of the rehearsal process. If you were a gymnast, you would work on your strength, agility and flexibility daily to ready yourself for competition. As a student of drama, you do the same with your imagination. Through the exercises in this chapter, you will start to harness the power of your imagination to create a logical world for the characters you are to play.

Actors today need to use their imaginations more than ever. As you start to work in TV and film, you will find yourself in a wide variety of locations, often having to imagine that you are somewhere completely different. With blue screen technology, you may be standing in a studio surrounded by crew, playing a character who is about to be overwhelmed by an oncoming tidal wave.

Often, I watch my four-year-old son create a whole world in his imagination with just a car and a cushion. In some respects, it's our innate ability to imagine that we as actors have to tap into.

AS, A2, IB,
BTEC National,
GCSE, KS3.

14 THE MAGIC IF

Student exercise

AIM

To use the magic if in a variety of circumstances.

- Find a space in the studio and sit down. Whatever the actual time is when you are about to start this exercise, imagine that you are a full twelve hours ahead, and that you have been in class for all that time. So, if you are sitting in class and it's 2 p.m. now, imagine it is 2 a.m. and you have been in class for an additional twelve hours. Say to yourself, 'What if I had been here for twelve hours, what would I be thinking and feeling?'.

  - Start to imagine your new circumstances using the magic if. If I was still in the drama studio, what would my surroundings now look like? If I was still here, what about my family – what would they be thinking? How will I get home?
  - Using if, question yourself, so that you start to imagine you are in the different circumstance and the effect this change is having on you.
  - Imagine that you are still in class, but now in a completely different part of the country. If you live in London, imagine you are now in Brighton, by the sea. Now that you live by the sea, imagine what you would do after the class has finished. Imagine your walk home with your changed location.
  - Now ask yourself, what if I was in New York? Imagine you are now on a school trip to New York to watch a number of Broadway plays and take part in actor workshops. Imagine the change in temperature, the flight over and the anticipation of the workshops you are going to take part in.

Remember to allow your imagination to work freely, without forcing anything.

- We will now change the circumstances: the year is 2022, and the world is a very different place. You are still in a class, but the threat of terrorist attacks permanently hangs over society. This year, there have been eleven attacks on schools and colleges by fundamentalist groups. You all have gas masks in case of attack. All public places now have a gas attack alarm.

  - Imagine you were halfway through the lesson. What if the gas alarm went off: what would you do?
  - Improvise the alarm going off and start to ask yourselves questions to trigger your imagination. Imagine how you would feel within the circumstances and allow your imagination to feed into your actions.

Notes for the student

Using the imagination should always start off at a gentle speed; don't try to rush your thoughts, but gently build on them. If you relax when using your imagination, your mind will start to help you out. If you force too much, the mind finds it much harder to work. When the gas alarm goes off, don't 'overreact'. Remember, this is an exercise to practise using your imagination and not a performance.

Notes for the teacher

This exercise starts students off on the path to using their imagination actively; by starting slowly, they can build up pictures of their surroundings and recent events. Watch for students who are obviously forcing their imagination and ask them to relax. Stanislavski advised his students to coax their imaginations rather than to force them. Suggest that students 'let go' and allow their imaginations to be free; remind them there is no right or wrong. With the group gas attack improvisation, it may be a good idea to do it a couple of times. If students start to 'show' as opposed to imagine, just remind them that this is not about telling the audience what they are thinking about, but about them practising using their imaginations truthfully within a set of given circumstances.

Student follow-on exercise: within a circumstance

In Table 3.1, there are five situations to imagine you are in.
Ask yourself – if I was in this situation what would I be thinking and doing? Then just let your imagination do the rest.

This follow-on exercise is for you to practise using your imagination to create pictures and impressions. By imagining yourself in different circumstances, you are flexing your ability to use your imagination. Don't sit down and say, 'now I'm going to imagine', but do bits here and there, slowly building as you go. While you are brushing your teeth think, 'what if I was in the Amazon basin right now, how would I be brushing my teeth', or, when eating lunch, imagine you are the mountaineer at base camp before the last big push to the summit.

Table 3.1
Imagination situations

Working on an oil rig in the North Sea
Professional trekker taking tour parties along the Amazon River
A fire fighter attacking an out-of-control blaze
A mountaineer on his third attempt to climb Everest
A 100-metre runner warming up for the Olympic final

15 VISUALIZATION OF AN OBJECT

Student exercise

AS, A2, IB,
BTEC National,
GCSE.

AIM

To focus your imagination actively, and to develop an ability to use the senses to guide the imagination.

- Find a space in the studio and stand in a relaxed position.
- Imagine you are a tree: decide on what type of tree you are (oak, horse chestnut, silver birch) and how old you are. Have an impression of how long you have stood in this place for – are you an oak tree dating back 400 hundred years, or a young tree still growing strong?
- Where are you? Are you in a forest surrounded by other trees, on the side of a mountain with a view of all the surrounding countryside or in a park looking down on a cricket pitch? What can you see? Imagine the view and how it has changed over the years.
- What can you hear? Can you hear birds singing or aeroplanes flying over? Can you hear the noise of squirrels jumping through your branches?
- What can you smell? The sweet smell of lavender from the meadow, or the rich smell of the sea on the wind?
- What can you feel? Your roots spread evenly beneath you, the nesting of birds in your branches, the swaying of your branches in the wind?
- Now imagine your past and the events you have seen over the course of your life. Seeing a battle rage before you, a storm bringing trees around you crashing down, a family picnicking in the shade of your branches. Or you could **visualize** a young boy playing on his bike, then returning from school, in his graduation robes from university, getting married, bringing home his first child, right up until, as an old man, he sits on the bench opposite and quietly reflects on his life.

visualizations
The pictures we see in our mind's eye.

Notes for the student

Stanislavski said the imagination works like a film reel, so, as you imagine, allow the pictures to start to blend into one another. Use detail to help: if you are looking out at the view, start by imagining close up and then move further away, slowly building up pictures as you go. Imagine a farmer walking his dog as the sun sets behind him. Imagine a rabbit scurrying to its burrow and birds flying through the sky. Allow the detail to build in your mind's eye, always remembering to stay relaxed and not to force anything.

By putting yourself in the position of the tree, you start to see life from the tree's point of view. Through the imagination, you have started to create a character for the tree. You have started to experience the life of the tree. When creating a character, you can transfer this exercise (and the others in the chapter) to help you create a rounded and active character.

This exercise extends to the 'Visualization 2' exercise as part of the acting exercise programme in Chapter 11, where you will also imagine your shape, size and texture.

Student follow-on exercise: using different objects

Choose one of the five objects below and follow the same process: concentrate on slowly building up pictures and creating detail.

- a castle
- a bridge
- a cathedral
- a mountain
- a glacier.

Start with your object in a different place/country from your tree, in a different climate and with a different view.

AS, A2, IB, BTEC National, GCSE, KS3.

16 USING THE SENSES

Student exercise

AIM

To slowly build up the use of the five senses.

The sky at night

- Sit on a chair in a space and slowly 'pull yourself up by the strings' – imagine that a thin wire runs from the base of your spine up through the top of your head to the ceiling (Figure 3.1). Imagine this is being

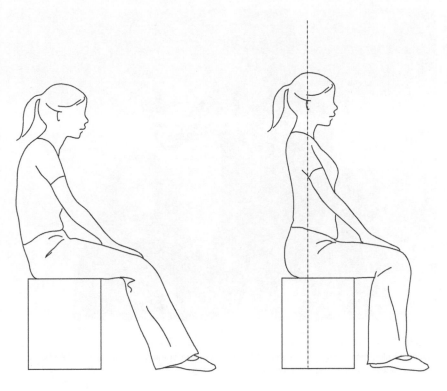

Figure 3.1
Pulled up by the strings.
Left: before; right: after

gently pulled; this should put you in a good physical position to start using your imagination.

- Imagine it is night-time and you are looking out at the stars in the sky.
- You can hear the trees blowing in the wind as you sit and look up at the stars.
- Keeping the picture of the stars and the sound of the wind in the trees, imagine the smell of lavender from a nearby bush.
- You take out a thermos flask from your bag, feeling the warmth in the cup as you pour.
- Taking a sip from the cup, you taste the rich hot chocolate on your tongue.
- Now, hold the impression of all five senses together for about thirty seconds.

The forest

- Sitting in a relaxed position, gently pull yourself up by the strings (Figure 3.2). Imagine you are in a forest, the forest is very old and you are alone. Imagine you are looking at the trees, their shapes and colour.

Figure 3.2
Student pulling herself up by the strings. Constance is imagining the string is pulling her up from the base of the spine, while I'm pulling the string

- You can smell the damp smell of the grass and moss from recent rainfall.
- You hear the scurrying of squirrels and the chirping of far off birds.
- Keeping an impression of the trees, the damp and the sounds of the forest, imagine pulling a sweet out of your pocket, the wrapper coming off in your hands and the sticky feel of the sweet.
- Imagine the taste of the toffee sweet filling your mouth and gently hold an impression of all of these together for about thirty seconds.

Notes for the teacher

For this exercise, you can choose a student to remind the others of the stimulus for the senses at each stage. It's always a good idea to go over each stimulus before the exercise, as there are always a couple of 'lavender – what does lavender smell like?' questions. As actors, they will always have to use their senses in unusual circumstances. If I was playing a soldier, I would need to imagine the smell of a spent rifle cartridge after I've shot my rifle. I may never have smelt this, but I can start to imagine the smell or imagine something very similar.

17 THE BEFORE-TIME

Student exercise

AS, A2, IB, BTEC National, GCSE.

- Look at Figure 3.3 and choose one of the characters. Work out your character's **before-time**, the events that lead up to this moment in the painting.
- Imagine what has happened that day, ending in the moment of the painting.
- Through your imagination, start to build pictures of where your character lives, what they do, how old they are, where they have just come from.
- As your character, walk through your life from your first memory up to the day of the painting.
- Who might they be looking at? Why is the girl on the right smiling?

Student follow-on exercise: in the car

- Now look at Figure 3.4 and choose one of the characters. Imagine what their life is like on a daily basis, where they work, where they live, how old they are and what they do in their spare time.
- Imagine your relationship with the other person in the painting; how do you know them? Are you married? Is it a first date? What has just happened?
- Start to imagine what you want (your objective) and what you are going to do to achieve it (your action).
- Remember always to imagine using pictures of the character's past, almost like a film strip as seen through their eyes.
- With a partner, set up two chairs to represent the car and freeze in the position of the painting, while imagining your character's before-time, the given circumstances, and your objective and action.

Notes for the student

This exercise is a variation on one of the exercises Stanislavski used when training actors towards the end of his life, at the Opera-Dramatic Studio in Moscow. The painting gives you a starting point to work back from and imagine what has happened before this moment. Try to put yourself in the position of the character and then imagine, so, if you are the driver of the car, imagine getting dressed in the morning and walking into work, going into a meeting and maybe getting a bagel and a coffee at lunch. I imagine the characters in the painting to be American, so my pictures become

AIM

To understand how to create the before-time of a character using your imagination.

before-time
The events leading up to the start of the play, or before each new entrance your character makes. Your character's life imagined actively from your first memory up to the start of the play.

Figure 3.3 *Two Women at a Window* by Bartolome Esteban Murillo

Figure 3.4 *In the Car* by Roy Lichtenstein

American, with my character living in New York. I imagine going for a walk in Central Park. It doesn't matter that I've never been there; I imagine I have, and anyway I've watched enough episodes of *Friends* to have a good idea of what it's like! Otherwise, I can have a look online for images or in a book about New York and filter those images into my imagination.

Performance tip

When watching students perform, the before-time, or lack of it, is one of the first things I notice. I will often stop a student after a few seconds and ask them what they, as the character, have just been doing. Or where they have come from. If the student has to think, they have not prepared their before-time correctly. In performance, it really stands out and is worth working on. Across the syllabi at AS, A2, IB and BTEC, you will be performing an extract from a play. When you come on stage, you need to have imagined, in detail, your before-time. Working on your before-time can be the difference between a rounded performance and one lacking depth.

You need also to imagine events that happen off stage in between your entrances. While playing Bruce Delamitri in *Popcorn*, after the first scene, I went off stage, put a dinner jacket on and then went back on stage to deliver my speech for winning an Oscar. The stage time was about two minutes, whereas, in real time, it was about twenty-four hours. During rehearsals, I needed to imagine the day of the Oscars, arriving on the red carpet, schmoozing with the big names and anticipating the decision on my film. If I hadn't imagined this when I came on stage to deliver the speech, my character would have been missing twenty-four hours of their life.

Notes for the teacher

This exercise allows students to start creatively using their imagination. You might want them to work together to create the before-time for the first painting and then, at home, prepare the character for the second painting. It would be good for the students to then come into the class and talk through the character they created at home. By doing this, you and the student will notice any holes or illogicalities that appear, and these can then be worked on by the student.

Teacher extension exercise: the old book

- *Seat the students in a circle, bring in an old book and place it in the middle of the circle.*
- *Give the students five minutes to create the book's before-time. Each student in turn stands up, picks up the book and tells the story of the book's*

before-time, where it was made, who owned it, the places it ended up, what it was used for.
- *Suggest that the students have no boundaries (within reason) to their stories, with the group voting at the end on the most believable story.*

18 THE SPACE AROUND YOU

AS, A2, IB, BTEC National, GCSE.

Student group exercise

AIM

To use your imagination to build the setting around you.

- As a group, all stand in a different space in the studio. You are now to imagine that you are all in a different part of a palace and its grounds. Have a quick look at the bird's-eye view of a palace in Figure 3.5, and then move to a different part of the studio, deciding which room or part of the grounds you are in.
- Move around the space, so that it's logical that where you are standing would correlate to a part of the palace or garden.
- One by one, describe what is around you, what you can see, hear, touch, taste and smell. Listen carefully to each other's description and picture it in your mind's eye as they talk.
- Once you have all described your room or part of the grounds, swap with the person next to you and see if you can recall and describe the room or part of the grounds as they had described them.

Notes for the student

By doing this exercise, you will start to imagine your surroundings. Plays are often set in one or two rooms, but you will have to create the rest of the house in your mind's eye. This means that, when you are standing on stage in one room, you have an impression of where all the other rooms are in the house. So, when you are talking about another character, in the study, your actions will be directed in that way, and the audience will understand. Often it's the little things that have an effect on the audience's understanding of the play. That's one of the reasons Stanislavski instilled a strict, disciplined work ethic in his actors, so that they didn't miss anything out in their preparation for a role.

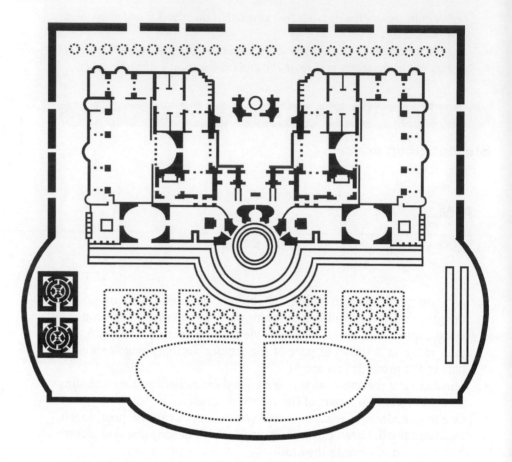

Figure 3.5
The palace

Teacher extension exercise: working in the palace

*Now that your students have the layout of the palace in their minds, give them
each a character from the list below and ask them, one by one, to walk through
the palace, as their character, as if it were a normal day. Ask them to imagine
the different rooms as they go and start to think about what their character
might be thinking within the circumstances they create.*

- *a palace cleaner*
- *a security guard*
- *the butler*
- *a lady in waiting*
- *a gardener*
- *a secretary*
- *a royal advisor.*

19 THE BEACH

Teacher-led exercise

AS, A2, IB,
BTEC National,
GCSE.

AIM

To be able to differentiate between using your imagination actively and using it passively.

- Sit in a chair pulling yourself up by the strings, shut your eyes; your teacher is now going to walk you through using your imagination in two different ways.
- So relax and gently start to imagine (Figure 3.6).
- Your teacher will say:

> You see yourself standing in a room; you see yourself bending to pick up a bag; you see yourself walking towards the door; you see yourself opening the door; you see yourself walking outside; you see yourself walking down the road; you see yourself looking out to sea; you see yourself walking on the sand; you see yourself putting down your bag; you see yourself taking out a towel; you see yourself lie down on the towel; you see yourself open your book; and you see yourself starting to read.

Now, keeping an impression of what that felt like, you will try using your imagination a different way (Figure 3.7).

You bend down and slowly pick up your yellow beach bag; you slide the bag on to your shoulder as you turn towards the glass door. Opening the door, you're hit by a wave of heat as you start to walk down the path. At the road, you turn left and you can feel the sun on your shoulders, you hear the hum of traffic and smell the salt in the air. After a while, you stop and wait for a gap in the traffic before crossing the road; you look out at the gorgeous blue expanse of sea; you see a tanker in the distance and hear birds circling above. At the beach, you stop and flick off your flip flops, feeling the warm sand in between your toes as you search for a spot to put your towel down. You hear a radio in the distance and the sound of children playing happily. You stop, put down your bag and take out your red beach towel. Lying down, you take out your book and start to read where you last left off.

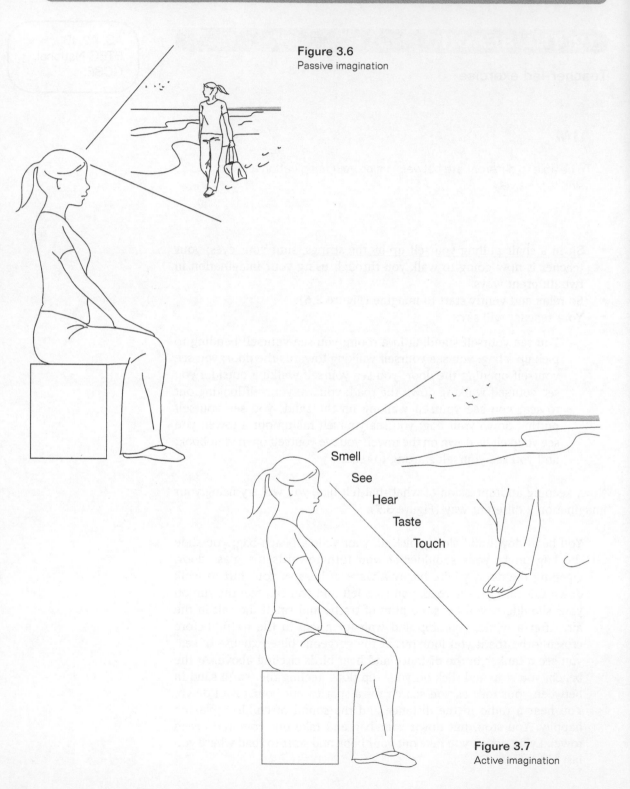

Figure 3.6
Passive imagination

Smell

See

Hear

Taste

Touch

Figure 3.7
Active imagination

Questions on the exercise

- Comparing the first and second time, was there any difference in the way you were using your imagination?
- Did it feel different when you were 'seeing yourself' do something from when you were imagining what you could see, hear, touch, taste and smell?
- Which was the easier for you to imagine, the first or second?
- Stanislavski said, 'We need an active not a passive imagination.'[2] Did the first one or the second one make you use your imagination actively?

Notes for the student

Active imagination is where we see things through our character's eyes, using the senses. **Passive imagination** is where we imagine what the audience thinks about what we are doing on stage. For example, Hamlet, looking at Gertrude, his mother, in active imagination may think, 'when I look at her I feel nothing but anger at how she betrayed my father's memory', or, with passive imagination, 'If I frown deeply then the audience will definitely know I'm not happy with my mother'.

This exercise is to give you an understanding of when you are using your imagination actively as the character and when you are not. When I am using my imagination to create the before-time of the character, I imagine everything as if through my character's eyes, as we did with the tree visualization exercise. So, if my character witnessed a battle, I would imagine the battle raging before me, rather than a picture of me in my head watching the battle.

If there is one thing you can guarantee before you go on stage, it's that you have every chance of slipping into using your imagination passively and worrying about what the audience will think of you. As actors, we need to be able gently to start to use our imaginations actively, so that we imagine our character within the circumstances of the play, with an objective and an action.

For many of us, we will naturally start to think about what the audience thinks about us. So, how do we make sure we start to use our imagination actively? Luckily, Stanislavski came up with something to help us use our imaginations actively, which will be looked at in the next chapter, on '**free body**'.

It's when we are using our imaginations actively that we start to really experience the character in a combination of the mind, body and spirit.

active imagination
Seeing things through our character's eyes, using the five senses.

passive imagination
Seeing ourselves from the audience's point of view while on stage.

free body
The desired state for an actor, a body free from tension, which can be used to create and experience a role.

Performance tip

Five minutes before you go on stage, stand in the wings and start to imagine what you can see, hear, touch, taste and smell as the character. Imagine what you want and what you are going to do to achieve it. Think about what you, as the character, think about the people in the next scene. Gently imagine all these things, and, when your cue comes, you'll be using your imagination actively.

Notes for the teacher

Students often react in different ways to this exercise, with some saying they found the first easier, some the second. The purpose of the exercise is really for them to see how they use their imagination and that, if they imagine watching themselves do something, it will become passive and, to make it more active, they need to imagine things through the character's eyes.

Student follow-on exercise: walking with pictures

Now, actually walk through going to the beach, imagining as you go. In the room you are in, actually pick up your bag, open the door and wait for the gap in the traffic, as well as allowing yourself to feel the heat on your shoulders and the wind on your face. Look out to sea and imagine you are going to run up and dive in.

Then, imagine it's winter and follow the same journey, but with it being cold and gloomy. Does the change in weather have an effect on your character?

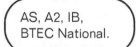

AS, A2, IB,
BTEC National.

20 MEMORY RECALL

Student exercise

AIM

To practise recalling memories to examine the emotion attached to the memory.

- Look at Table 3.2 and try to recall a memory for each one.
- For some, the memory may come easily; if not, move onto the next one and come back to it later.
- Once you have found the memory, slowly recall until you can feel the emotion that is attached to the memory. Keep an impression of what the emotion feels like, so you can draw on this when needed in the rehearsal process.
- Remember, we can only recall memories gently; any forcing will have the opposite effect, and you'll find it more difficult to recall a memory.
- Once you have recalled the emotion and you have an impression of what it was like, you can use that emotion within a given circumstance.

Student extension exercise: adding emotion

- In twos or threes, choose one memory from the list in Table 3.2 and create a scenario around it using the emotions from the memory recall. For example:

  - You are on a first date and are anxious to impress. You met in a seminar at university. The other day you bumped into each other at the library, got chatting and now you're out on a date. Bring in the impression of what it felt like for you when you were on a first date and use that with the character you are creating.

Notes for the student

This exercise is meant to trigger memories that can supply you, as the student, with an understanding of an emotion. It's not about trawling through your subconscious trying to locate personal or painful memories. Keep the exercise nice and light, with the emphasis on experiencing an emotion.

21 EMOTION MEMORY

Student exercise

AIM

To start to use a memory from the past to aid you, the actor, within the rehearsal process.

Table 3.2
Memories to recall

A first date

A terrifying encounter

Winning something

Hearing bad news

Being stood up

Feeling anger at someone

Having done something wrong

Being in a hurry and searching for something

Arguing with someone you care about

Being jealous

AS, A2, IB, BTEC National.

- Think back over your life to a time when you felt fear. It could have been when you'd done something wrong and thought you'd be found out, or it may have been a time when you were somewhere you shouldn't have been and thought you were going to get caught.
- In pairs, describe your memories to each other, trying to remember what you were thinking at the time and how you felt about it. Don't choose something too personal; this is not about you sharing your inner thoughts, but describing a memory and what you felt at the time.
- Look at the following bit from Ibsen's *A Doll's House*. Krogstadt has left a letter addressed to Nora's husband in the locked letterbox. Information damaging to Nora is in the letter, and only her husband has a key. Nora knows that, when her husband opens the letterbox, he will find the letter and discover that Nora had borrowed money by forging the signature of her father.

Nora	In the letterbox! [*she creeps stealthily across to the hall door*] There it is! Torvald, Torvald! It's hopeless now!
Mrs Linde	[*comes into the room, left, carrying a costume*] There, I think that's everything. Shall we try it on?
Nora	[*in a low, hoarse whisper*] Kristine, come here.
Mrs Linde	[*throws the dress down on the sofa*] What's wrong with you? You look upset.
Nora	Come here. Do you see that letter? There, look! Through the glass in the letterbox.
Mrs Linde	Yes, yes I can see it.
Nora	It's a letter from Krogstad.
Mrs Linde	Nora! It was Krogstad who lent you the money!
Nora	Yes. And now Torvald will get to know everything.
Mrs Linde	Believe me, Nora, it's best for you both.
Nora	But there's more to it than that. I forged a signature . . .
Mrs Linde	Heavens above!

A Doll's House, in *Four Major Plays*, Henrik Ibsen,
Oxford World Classics, 2008. By permission
of Oxford University Press.[3]

- Improvise the scene, drawing on your memories of fear to understand how Nora felt within these circumstances. Use the feeling from your memories as a way in to how Nora may have been feeling.

Notes for the student

Emotion memory, like much of the system, is a tool to help you, the student, during the rehearsal process. It's to be used when rehearsing and then 'let go of' well before going on stage. Stanislavski never intended that actors would be on stage remembering past experiences to create an emotion in front of an audience. If something upsets you as a person, then that should not be used during the rehearsal process to create a character. By dragging up upsetting memories during rehearsals, you will only distract yourself from your real goal of experiencing your character on stage.

Notes for the teacher

There is often a degree of confusion between Stanislavski's system and the Method born out of America. In many ways, the Method is an 'Americaniza-tion' of the system that suits both the American actor and American culture. Perhaps the thing to remember is that emotion memory was only meant to enhance the actor's understanding of an emotion during rehearsal and then 'left alone', and was never meant to be relived before an audience. Stanislavski believed the rehearsal room was no place for psychoanalysis, and I try to follow his lead, keeping discussion and analysis related to the given circumstances.

22 LIFE IN ART

AS, A2, BTEC National, undergraduate.

Student group extension exercise

AIM

To put into practice the skills learned in the first three chapters, using objectives, actions and imagination together.

- Figure 3.8 is a painting by Renoir; there are fourteen characters in the painting and therefore fourteen parts. If you have more students in your group, you can double up, and, if fewer, you can only choose the characters in the foreground.
- Start by as a group deciding on:
  - where you are;
  - who you are;
  - when it is;
  - why you are there;
  - how you came to be there.

Figure 3.8
Luncheon of the Boating Party by Pierre-Auguste Renoir

- You will probably need to research Renoir and the historical period he painted in.
- Then, individually, imagine the before-time of your character from their first memory to the day of the painting.
- As a group, share your findings on your character and create an agreed set of given circumstances.
- Now, decide on an objective and action for each of your characters, leading up to the painting.
- Improvise the minute leading into the painting and then freeze.
- You can also find costumes and basic props to add authenticity to the scene.
- Then, show the scene to your teacher and see what they think!

Notes for the student

This exercise has brought together the skills learned in these first three chapters and is a chance for you to create and experience a role. Afterwards, look back at the process and see what worked and what didn't. Did you use your imagination actively? Did you have a clear action or actions that helped you to achieve your objective? If you are unsure, go back to the relevant chapter and go over the student exercises at home to help. Remember that, by experiencing and evaluating, you will start to build an understanding of how to use Stanislavski's system – it's not about you getting it right, but rather you experiencing the role within a set of circumstances and enjoying it!

Notes for the teacher

I would use this exercise to give students the chance to put into practice the skills they have learned over the last three chapters. This will help students to position the various elements of their system in their mind and start to help them to understand how they connect together.

I appreciate that, for many of you, time is of the essence, with busy syllabi to accomplish, so why not choose one main exercise on objectives, actions and imagination, with the student exercises to be done at home, working towards this 'Life in art' exercise. This would then work as a solid platform on which to build the text work, as required by the syllabi. When I think about this exercise, I can see that Stanislavski wanted his students to appreciate 'art' as a form, and he knew the importance of introducing students to as many art media as possible, to encourage their imaginations and analytical antennae. This will also give you the opportunity to observe your students starting to use the system in a very practical way, which will help to demystify and highlight the usefulness of the system to the student of drama.

IMAGINATION

Imagination is the actor's ability to treat fictional circumstances as if they were real.

Visualizations are the pictures we see in our mind's eye.

As actors, we use our imagination to visualize everything, from the circumstances of the play, what we want, how we will achieve it, our character's past, to the events of the play.

Stanislavski wanted us to use our imaginations actively so that we can experience the 'I am being' of the character.

When visualizing the character's past, our imaginations work like a film reel, linking together pictures and impressions of events as they happened.

4 Free body

Free body is often the part of the Stanislavski system that students overlook, but, for me, free body is one of the most important elements for the student of drama. It is only when you have a free body that you can fully use your imagination and be 'free' on stage. Throughout my life as an actor, I have been aware of the benefits of relaxation, but it was not until I started running workshops that I saw firsthand the effect it really has on the actor's performance.

A few years ago, I was running a workshop and decided to do a simple acting exercise followed by a full free-body relaxation, and then the students would perform the exercise again. The idea was that they would compare the first exercise with the second (after the relaxation) to see if it had made any difference. I was really surprised at the difference the relaxation had made to the group's attention, focus, imagination and freedom of movement. I remember the teacher, who had been catching up on some paperwork, stopped during the repeat of the exercise and stared open mouthed. She said afterwards that their focus almost pulled her in and she couldn't stop watching the students' work. I too was amazed at the difference in the students' work after the free-body relaxation. I have used free-body relaxation across the country, with a wide variety of students, always to positive reaction, ranging from 'was that magic?' in East London to 'I want to kiss you' in Brighton!

I now use this exercise as an integral part of any Stanislavski workshop, and I recommend you, as a student of drama, use the 'Relaxation' exercise in this chapter as a cornerstone of your drama development.

AS, A2, IB, BTEC National.

23 PHYSICAL TENSIONS

Teacher-led exercise

AIM

To understand how tension affects our ability to think and imagine.

- Find a space and get into a press-up position. Hold the position for ten seconds; make sure you are rigid and try not to let your body sag. Your teacher will now ask you to perform three tasks; try to do them the best you can:

  - imagine the taste of an orange;
  - recall the smell of coffee;
  - imagine the touch of leather.

- Now find a chair, sit down and relax. Again, your teacher will ask you to:

  - imagine the taste of an orange;
  - recall the smell of coffee;
  - imagine the touch of leather.

- Was it easier the second time or the first time? How did being tense affect the way you could remember and work something out?
- Stanislavski said, 'There can be no question of true, subtle feeling or of the normal psychological life of a role while physical tension is present.'[1] What do you think he meant? What does this tell us about the tensions we have as actors?

Notes for the student

Hopefully, this exercise showed you how difficult it can be to think and imagine when you are tense. Tension often comes out of nerves; many actors are most nervous just before they go on stage.

Stanislavski used free-body relaxation with his actors to help deal with the tensions caused by nerves and the tensions that we have built up over the course of our lives, many of which we are unaware of. Our job is to locate these tensions and then start to work on relaxing them. If, for example, you have tense shoulders, every part you play will have tense shoulders. Therefore, as a drama student, you have to learn to relax the tension in your shoulders before you start to create a character.

Student follow-on exercise: observing tensions

Over the next few days, observe the tensions you have and other people have. Observe how, as people get older, their tensions become more obvious. If you locate a tension you have now, imagine living with that tension for another fifty years and how it would affect your life. When you think you've found a part of the body that is tense, slowly relax it and watch to see if, over the next couple of days, it makes any difference.

Notes for the teacher

If there is a chorus of moans at being made to take a press-up position, tell students they should think themselves lucky – Stanislavski got his students to pick up the piano! I also remind students that actors need to be physically fit and strong and have complete control over their bodies. In this chapter, there is a section on yoga that will come in handy for the less physically confident of students. This exercise starts to bring an awareness of the role tensions play in acting and the effect they have on what we can think and do.

AS, A2, IB,
BTEC National,
GCSE.

24 THE TENSIONS IN OTHERS

Student exercise

AIM

To observe the tensions in others, while carrying out simple tasks. This will help you to start noticing the tensions in yourself.

Paired student exercise

- One of you will be the observer, while the other one carries out a number of physical tasks.
- The observer's job is to watch for any physical tensions and point them out, while the other student carries out the tasks.
- The student carrying out the tasks then checks for physical tensions and starts to relax them.
- Often, just an awareness of a tension will mean you can start to relax that tension.
- Here's a list of physical activities:

    - Walk at different speeds from one side of the room to the other.
    - Take everything out of your bag and put it back.
    - Unstack some chairs and then restack them.
    - Pick up a number of costumes and put them at different points around the drama studio.
    - Open and shut the door.

Notes for the student

The observer tries to spot when the student is using too much tension to do the given activity. If you think they are tense, tell them where you think the tension is – for example, in their shoulders, hands, neck.

The student carrying out the activity can then check and can start to build up an awareness of when they use tensions, so they can relax them.

We all have tensions that we carry around with us each day and don't even realize. This exercise helps to us to start to understand where the tensions exist so that we can relax them.

Often, it's in people's hands that we see tensions. When you are next watching people being interviewed on television, have a look at their hands and see if they are unnaturally tense.

25 THE TENSIONS IN US

Student individual exercise

AS, A2, IB, BTEC National, GCSE.

AIM

For the student to work on growing an awareness of how their body moves and the tensions present during movement.

The cat

- Follow the basic movements of a cat. Start curled up on the floor, then slowly spread out, imagining each of your four limbs is one of the limbs of a cat.
- Come up on to all fours and roll your neck around.
- Slowly move forward and then stretch your spine, keeping your arms stretched out in front of you and your head down.
- Arch your back, pushing up on to your fingers and toes.

Notes for the student

This exercise can be done at home so that you can start to observe the different parts of your body at work. As you move, think about how your limbs are working and try to use the correct amount of tension for the movement. When you next see a cat, observe the fluidity of its movements and try to do the same when you do this exercise.

Mission impossible

- You are on a mission and have two minutes to get through the next room before the alarm goes off. There is a network of invisible lasers that will trigger off the alarm system if you cross them.
- You have an infrared device that, when switched on, shows up where the lasers are.
- You have to move across the room going under, over, around and in between the lasers.
- You will need to stretch out and contract your body, all the time keeping an awareness of the tensions you are using.

Notes for the student

Imagine you have an internal tension register that scans your body, identifies any tension and starts to relax it. By doing exercises like this, you are building up an awareness of your own body and an ability to relax. Combined with the 'Relaxation' exercise, you will soon start to notice a tension and relax the tension automatically.

Performance tip

Five minutes before you are about to go on stage, scan your body for tensions and relax any you find. By going through this process, you will also start to focus your mind and body ready for performance.

AS, A2, IB,
BTEC National,
GCSE.

26 THE PLAYROOM

Group exercise

AIM

To be aware of tensions when moving and to start to introduce the tensions of the character.

- Imagine that the drama studio is now a child's play area and you are all children's toys.

- Choose a toy from the list:

  - a rag doll
  - Barbie
  - Action Man
  - a teddy bear.

- Imagine that, when the boy or girl, whose room it is, has left the room you come alive.
- Imagine the physical tensions that your toy would need to move.
- Start to move around the room, remembering to relax your tensions but bring in the tensions of your toy.
- Using your imagination, allow yourself to picture what is around you and the size of the room in relation to your size as the toy. For most rooms, the ceiling is twice as high as the average person, but for Barbie the average ceiling would be ten times higher.
- Think about how the plastic used to make Barbie would make her move in contrast to the soft stuffing of a teddy bear.
- As you move around, imagine what your toy would be doing if they came to life and what they might want. Action Man might start getting all his kit together, and Barbie might be deciding on what dress to wear next.

Notes for the student

After the exercise, think about how you moved and how the toy's natural tensions affected your movement. Think about your tensions as the actor and how you had to relax them before taking on the tensions of your toy. With an exercise like this, you can start to bring in other areas of the system you have already learned. This will help you, as the actor, to start to piece together how the elements of the system work together in practice.

Notes for the teacher

Give the students a bit of time to create the world of the playroom and start to move around as the toy. This exercise gives the student confidence to move around the space, concentrating on the tensions of the toy while using their imagination. Encourage students to start using areas of the system they have already worked on, so that they can have an objective and an action, while visualizing the objects around them.

AS, A2, IB,
BTEC National,
GCSE.

27 RELAXATION

Teacher-led exercise

AIM

To understand the process of relaxing the mind and body.

- Imagine you are an artist, you have just been to the Lake District for inspiration and are now back in your studio. Imagine the easel in front of you and the paintbrush in your hand. You are going to paint, from memory, a landscape you observed (Figure 4.1). Your objective is 'I want to do my best', and the action is 'I enjoy'. Your teacher will stop you after thirty seconds and ask you to lie down on the floor and follow their instructions. Keep an impression of what it was like using your imagination and if you managed to stay focussed as the painter during those thirty seconds.

- Now, lie on your back, place your legs about shoulder-width apart and your arms by your side, with your palms facing up (Figure 4.2). Make sure your spine and neck are in a straight line and close your eyes. Your teacher or another student will now talk you through the relaxation.

Figure 4.1
Painting, pre-relaxation

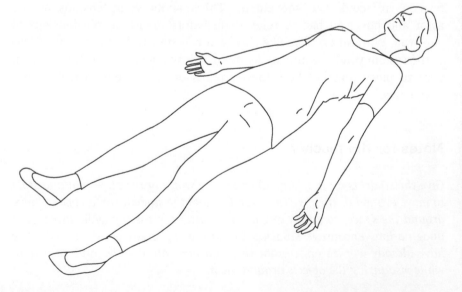

Figure 4.2
Relaxation

Breath in	Breath out
Breath in	Breath out
Breath in	Breath out
I am relaxing my toes	my toes are completely relaxed
I am relaxing my feet	my feet are completely relaxed
I am relaxing my ankles	my ankles are completely relaxed
I am relaxing my calves	my calves are completely relaxed
I am relaxing my knees	my knees are completely relaxed
I am relaxing my thighs	my thighs are completely relaxed
I am relaxing my hips	my hips are completely relaxed
I am relaxing my stomach	my stomach is completely relaxed
I am relaxing my chest	my chest is completely relaxed
I am relaxing my lower back	my lower back is completely relaxed
I am relaxing my spine	my spine is completely relaxed
I am relaxing my upper back	my upper back is completely relaxed
I am relaxing my shoulders	my shoulders are completely relaxed
I am relaxing my upper arms	my upper arms are completely relaxed
I am relaxing my elbows	my elbows are completely relaxed
I am relaxing my lower arms	my lower arms are completely relaxed
I am relaxing my hands	my hands are completely relaxed
I am relaxing my fingers	my fingers are completely relaxed
I am relaxing my neck	my neck is completely relaxed
I am relaxing my head	my head is completely relaxed
I am relaxing my face	my face is completely relaxed
I am relaxing my eyes	my eyes are completely relaxed
I am relaxing my cheeks	my cheeks are completely relaxed
I am relaxing my mouth	my mouth is completely relaxed
PAUSE	
I am relaxing my mind	my mind is completely relaxed

Allow the students to relax for a minute or two (Figure 4.3).

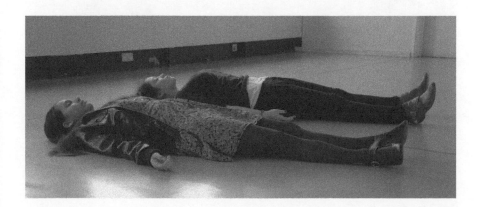

Figure 4.3
Students relaxing.
Constance and Amber are
about halfway through the
'Relaxation' exercise

- Slowly stand up, first by getting up to your knees and completely in your own time, and then return to your chair.
- Now imagine you are the artist again, you have just been to the Lake District for inspiration and are now back in your studio. Imagine the easel in front of you and the paintbrush in your hand. You are going to paint from memory a landscape you observed. Your objective is 'I want to do my best', and the action is 'I enjoy' (Figure 4.4).

Questions for after the exercise

- Was there a difference between the first and the second time you did the exercise?
- If so, what was the difference?
- Did the relaxation help you to imagine actively the second time?
- Describe to the class how the relaxation felt and compare your experience.

Notes for the student

Students often say the relaxation was like 'sinking into the floor', and they could feel each part of their body relax as the relaxation went on. Often, you will find during the first painting exercise your focus wavers, but after the relaxation you can really focus, your imagination seems to flow and 'you just know what to paint'.

Figure 4.4
Students painting after relaxation. Both students are painting after the relaxation, with their attention on what they are painting and not what else is happening around them

Many times, I have watched a room full of students turn into a room full of artists after free-body relaxation! This is why we do relaxation; it helps us, as actors, move from thinking about what the audience thinks of us, to imagining what our character is thinking and doing. It helps the actor to move from a passive imagination to a more active imagination.

Student follow-on exercise: practising relaxation

You can start to practise relaxation at home. Simply lie on the floor and go through each part of the body, as I have done above. Just say it in your mind and relax. The more you practise, the more you relax. Eventually, you will be sitting outside the casting room waiting for your audition and you will say 'I am relaxing my mind, my mind is completely relaxed' and you'll start to relax.

Performance tip

Before each performance, find a quiet space and, during the half (the half hour before you go on stage), take a few minutes to relax. Go through the relaxation above and then slowly start to imagine your character's past, the before-time, the circumstances of the first scene, your objective and action.

Notes for the teacher

I've written the relaxation out in full, so that, the first couple of times, you can read it off the page. I go quite slowly and speak in a quiet voice, creating a calm atmosphere, and observe the students as they relax. Often, you can see parts of the body visibly relaxing, and it helps to point out to students where you have seen them visibly relax. Later, they can think back over the relaxation and recall that moment. There will always be a couple of students who find it difficult at first and fight the relaxation; for them, I recommend they practise at home, and soon it will be much easier. At the same time, there are students who completely embrace the relaxation and afterwards look completely calm. I would recommend doing this free-body relaxation at the start of lessons and rehearsal period and with AS, A2, IB and BTEC groups. It's good practice for them to take it in turns to run the relaxation and observe each other relaxing. With the more challenging GCSE groups, relaxation can work wonders.

AS, A2, IB,
BTEC National,
GCSE, KS3.

28 YOGA

Student exercises

AIM

To start to relax your mind and body to create a calm state to begin
your work on a character

- Find yourself a space in the drama studio or at home.
- I have outlined some yoga postures for you to start your practice with.
  You can work through them in order, remembering to pay attention to
  your breathing and relaxing in the postures.

Downward dog – Adho Mukha Svanasana (Figure 4.5)

- Go on to your hands and knees, with your wrists underneath your
  shoulders and knees underneath hips.
- Straighten your legs and push back, so you raise your hips.
- Spread your fingers wide.
- Let your head hang down.
- Try to slowly sink your heels down to the floor.
- Breathe in and breathe out, allowing your attention to move to
  allowing your heels to slowly reach the floor.

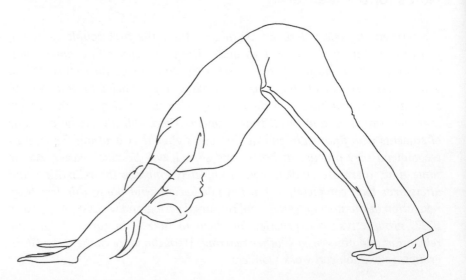

Figure 4.5
Downward dog

- Push up with your legs to take the weight off your arms and relax into the pose.

Warrior I – Virabhadrasana (Figure 4.6)

- Start in downward facing dog and move your right foot up next to your right hand.
- Turn your left foot away from you at an angle of 45°, pivoting on the ball of your foot.
- Bend your right knee to a 45° angle.
- Move your right hip back and your left hip forward, so that your hips are facing forward.
- Lift your arms up so that they are above your head and your palms are touching.
- Look up at your hands and concentrate on your breathing and holding the position.
- After about five breaths, go from this position back into the downward dog pose and do exactly the same, but for your left-hand side.

Figure 4.6
Warrior 1

Figure 4.7
Forward bend seated

Figure 4.8
Forward bend straddle

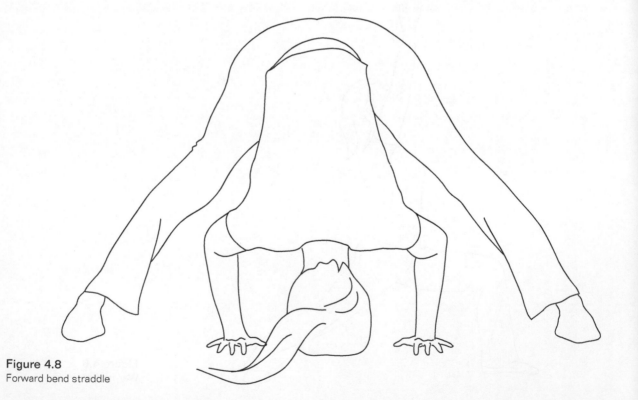

Forward bend seated – Paschimottanasana (Figure 4.7)

- Sit up straight, with your legs together in front of you.
- Lift your arms up, stretching them above your head.
- Breathe in, stretching out your spine.
- Breathe out and stretch forward, keeping the spine straight.
- With each breath, try to extend the spine, resting your hands on your ankles. Try to move your chest and tummy closer to your legs.
- Remember to keep your back straight as you reach for your ankles.

Standing forward bend straddle – Prasarita Padottanasana (Figure 4.8)

- Stand with your feet wide apart with your toes slightly pointing in.
- Slowly bend forward, keeping your spine straight.
- Put your hands on the floor in line, directly under your shoulders, and start walking them back so they are in line with your feet.
- Bend your elbows so they are facing towards your knees.
- Gently move your weight on to the balls of your feet and pull up by the legs.
- Breathe in and out and stay in the pose for around ten breaths, before slowly moving out of the pose.

Notes for the student

Use these postures as a foundation for your practice and enrol in a yoga class to learn and experience new postures. Start with a beginner's class and practise the new postures you learn at home.

The tensions we have in our body are relaxed through yoga. Yoga is the combination of the mind, spirit and body, and so, by doing yoga postures, we relax the mind, spirit and body to create a calm state to begin our work on a character. Yoga allows the actor to experience the flow of energy that creates the perfect state on which to build a character.

Performance tip

On the day of a performance, get up a bit earlier and practise yoga, relaxing your mind and body as you go through the postures. This will put you in the perfect state of mind for the performance. I would recommend doing the same on the day of a written exam too!

Stanislavski, throughout his life, was fascinated by yoga and the benefits for the actor. Unfortunately, because of Soviet censorship, many of his thoughts on yoga were not made readily available. We do know that Stanislavski practised yoga with his students, as part of their training, and today yoga is practised in many drama schools and colleges.

Notes for the teacher

It may be a good idea to practise a posture at the start of each lesson. I ran a workshop in a school in High Wycombe, and the drama teacher, as part of the course on Stanislavski at A level, introduced the students to a new yoga posture each lesson. After three lessons, they were excited to learn a new posture, and they were thoroughly enjoying the experience. This seemed an excellent way of introducing yoga to students and a great way to focus and energize students for the lesson. It's a good idea for students to be in easy clothes for the lesson.

AS, A2, IB,
BTEC National,
GCSE.

29 MEDITATION

Student exercise

AIM

To refresh your mind and body and observe the mind, body and spirit in harmony.

- Sit upright in a chair, remembering to pull yourself up by the strings.
- Rest your hands on your thighs, palms facing up, with the index finger and middle finger touching your thumb (Figure 4.9).
- Relax your jaw and breathe in through your nose.
- Close your eyelids and focus on your eyelids for thirty seconds.
- Start repeating 'om', as in hOMe, as if it were a sound you were sending up to your mind. As you inhale and exhale, repeat 'om' in time with your breathing.
- After a while, the 'om' will become what is called in yoga a silent sound. It will be as if the sound exists in your head, but you are no longer aware of it.
- Keep repeating 'om' for approximately ten minutes.

- Return the focus of your eyes to your eyelids for thirty seconds, and then your meditation is complete.

Notes for the student

Try this meditation at the end of your class. You can have one person keeping an eye on the time to let the others know when the ten minutes is up. Think about how you felt before the meditation and how you felt after. Did the meditation help energize you?

Meditation can help to refresh your mind and body, which could be most useful during your busy years of study. Try meditation at home, observing the affect it has on you.

Like all the exercises in this book, it is for you to experience and then decide if it helps you as an actor. If it does, then you can use it; if it doesn't – you haven't really lost anything by trying it out!

Figure 4.9
Meditation

FREE BODY

Free body is the term given to the desired state an actor should be in for performance.

Free body is when we, as actors, have a body free from tension and stress, which we can use to create and experience a role.

As actors, we are all striving to have a free body, for 'physical tension paralyses our whole capacity for action, our dynamism'.[2]

The tensions we have can be divided into two types: tensions that we have built up unknowingly over the course of our lives, and tensions that come from the circumstances we are in.

5 Communication

Stanislavski believed that we give off **rays** of **communication**, and it's these rays that represent what we are feeling and thinking. Rays are how we communicate when we're not speaking or doing anything with our bodies.

If you think back over your life, you'll probably be able to find a moment when you have communicated with another person without ever saying or doing anything.

A good example of communicating with rays is the first kiss. Years ago, I'd been out for a meal with a girl, and we had just got dropped off by the taxi. We were laughing and walking to the front door and then we stopped, and I kissed her. She then said, 'How did you know that was the exact moment I wanted you to kiss me?' Afterwards, I thought: it's because she told me, sending to me that she wanted me to kiss her. What she wanted was sent to me as a ray, and I picked it up. Probably, if we didn't have these rays as a species, we would have died out years ago!

It's this communication or radiation of feelings that is present around us all the time, and, as actors, we need to be able to harness it and use it on stage.

Stanislavski said, 'Communication through the mind constitutes one of the most important dynamic actions in acting and should be valued. It is absolutely essential in the process of creating and emitting the "life of the human spirit" of a role.'[1]

As actors, we communicate with other actors on stage as the character. We also have the job of communicating our character to the audience. As well as having an objective, an action and using our imagination, we have to communicate all this to the audience.

Imagine how it would feel performing to an empty house. It would be pointless; the actor needs an audience. As actors, we need to make sure that our character is understood by the audience. This is done by communication – it is you, the actor, sharing your character with the audience so that they can enjoy it. Almost like an indirect communication – 95 per cent of your attention goes on to the character within the circumstance, with 5 per cent making sure the audience sees, hears and understands what you are doing.

30 SENDING AND RECEIVING RAYS

Student exercise

AIM

To practise sending and receiving rays in preparation for developing stage relationships.

- Choose a partner, someone you feel relaxed with, and sit opposite them (Figure 5.1). Sit so your knees are level and about six inches apart. Rest your hands on your thighs and look into each other's eyes. Decide who is to be the sender and who is to be the receiver.
- The sender goes first. Think of a physical act for the other person to do, e.g. scratching an ear, folding their arms, touching their nose. You then need to transmit this to the receiver using rays, without forcing or tensing

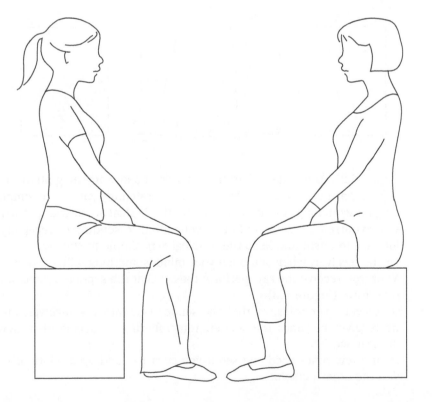

Figure 5.1
Preparing to send and receive

Figure 5.2
Sending rays

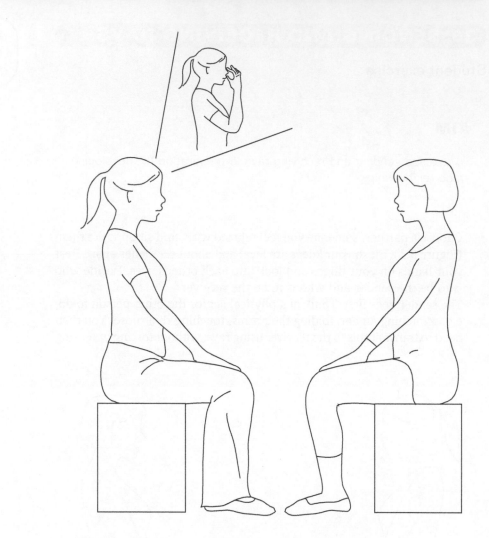

(Figure 5.2). Allow the rays to flow and don't show anything physically to your partner. So if you have chosen scratching your nose simply imagine scratching your nose and send this physical act to your partner.

- Allow yourself to relax, and open your mind to sending or receiving; don't try to push; and keep the physical acts simple to start with.
- For the receiver, when you open your mind, something will just pop in.
- When you receive the ray, perform the act that the sender wanted you to perform (Figure 5.3).
- Now swap over roles, so that the sender becomes the receiver, and the receiver becomes the sender, remembering to decide on a new physical act.
- Try it a few times each and see if you start to build up a relationship with the other person.

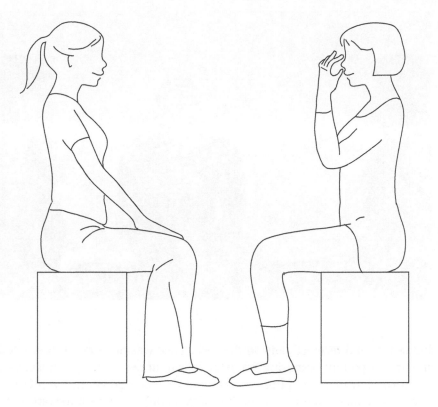

Figure 5.3
Receiving rays

- Now change partners and see if there is a difference with another person.

Notes for the student

I recently did this exercise with a group of BTEC National students at a school in Oldbury. We had just done the exercise 'Guilty or innocent', from later in this chapter, and talked a bit about invisible rays. Two girls went up to do this exercise: they sat down, looked each other in the eye, and then the receiver scratched her nose. The sender went bright red and stared open mouthed at the receiver. There was a silence, and I asked the sender if scratching her nose was the act she sent. She said it was, and both girls looked at each other in shock. Later, driving back from Birmingham, I thought about that moment. For the students, some 'Stanislavski guy' had come up from London and was telling them that we send and receive invisible rays. They looked at me, and I could see they were thinking, 'if these rays are invisible, how do we know they exist?'. This exercise worked so well, I didn't need to say any more; we had all experienced invisible rays

Figure 5.4
Students sending and receiving. Amber is sending to Constance. If you look closely, you can see Amber send and Constance open her mind in anticipation to receive. If you think you can't see anything, practise a few times with your partner, then come back and take another look.

being sent and received, and so their existence was now fact. It reminded me how important practising Stanislavski is to understanding Stanislavski. So, if you have just read this exercise, put the book down, find a partner, friend or sibling and give it a go. Even if you don't get it right to start with, by doing this exercise you will start to understand how rays work and how they work for the actor.

For this exercise to work, you need to take it seriously and focus fully. There may be a temptation to laugh, especially when looking directly into someone else's eyes. If you can have a disciplined approach to exercises in the studio, it will be a lot easier to keep a disciplined approach on stage. When I was in Moscow, I went to a number of workshops with Russian drama school students. One of the first things I noticed was their discipline. When they were given an exercise to do, they gave it their all. I was fascinated to see how Stanislavski's work ethic was still very evident in the students. The acting profession is highly competitive; for those of you wanting to enter the profession and to succeed at drama school, adopting a disciplined approach to your studies now will benefit you in the long run.

Student follow-on exercise: observing communication

Over the next couple of days, watch for communication and radiation in various situations with other people. At the end of the day, look back and see where there was an invisible communication between you and other people. In conversations, observe how much you pick up from speech, how much from body language and how much from rays.

Notes for the teacher

Students often take a bit of time to get used to this exercise, looking for immediate results, which won't necessarily come. Remind the student that this exercise is about experiencing the sending and receiving of rays, and this is the start of a process they will use when rehearsing or on stage. Some students will naturally work very well together, and others won't. For this exercise, it is best if students who already have a positive relationship or affinity work together.

Teacher extension exercise: picking up the rays

If you find a pair who work well together, you can set them this extension exercise to allow their communication skills to grow:

- *Have one student stand in front of the other student. Ask them both to relax. The student standing behind the first student will be the guide.*
- *The guide will not speak nor gesture, but use rays to let the person in front know what to do.*
- *The student in front only moves when they feel they are being instructed to move from the person behind.*
- *Tell the student at the back to keep it simple, for example walk forward, bend down, clap, go over and touch the wall.*
- *The student at the front should try to relax, clear their mind and be open to receiving. If something pops into their minds to do, that's probably the instruction being communicated.*
- *The rest of the group can watch and then comment.*
- *Once the two students have finished, ask the guide if the student at the front had done what they were communicating them to do.*

Notes for the student

When we were running exercises to be photographed (Figure 5.5), the photographer asked me to get in shot, while Connie and Amber did the exercise. I stood there and thought: I'll see what Connie's sending. So I opened my mind and, whatever came in, I did. I walked forward, clapped and turned around. Amber turned around and said that she didn't get anything. Connie laughed and said, 'You didn't, but Nick did.' Probably

Figure 5.5
Extension exercise: sending and receiving. Constance is sending and Amber receiving, with me joining in to see what I can receive – and obviously missing out on the joke. As you get better at sending and receiving, you'll be surprised at how much you can communicate this way

because there was no pressure on me to receive, I was relaxed, opened my mind and could easily pick up on Connie's rays. Connie and Amber practised these exercises a number of times; after a while, they would just look at each other and instantly send and receive. I teach an acting class that Amber is in and, every so often, mid class, I will look at her and realize she is sending me something – I think she wants to make sure I'm still on the ball!

AS, A2, IB,
BTEC National.

31 IMPROVISING WITH RAYS

Student exercise

AIM

For the student to start using rays within a given set of circumstances.

Two-person improvisation

- You are the husband and you have been married for five years. You play golf and have been booked to play in a tournament this weekend.

You are meant to be away from Friday evening until Sunday night. On the second tee this morning, you over-swung and you've put your back out. Instead of staying in the hotel, you decide to come home early, so you get in the car and head home. When you pull up, there is already a car in the drive. You don't recognize the car and go to the front door; opening the door, you walk in to see your wife's startled expression. You ask whose car it is, and she asks why you're back so early. You ask her whose car it is, and your wife replies that it's a friend from work. The improvisation will start at this point. Your immediate reaction is that she must be having an affair: the car is a sports car and must belong to one of the guys she works with; your back is very painful after the journey. Your action is 'I accuse'.

- You are the wife, your husband has had the golf weekend booked for ages, and you've been really looking forward to time on your own. You decide to go out with work friends on the Friday evening, and you all end up having quite a few drinks, and they come back to your house afterwards. One of the guys, Tony, has always been a bit flirty with you, but you never thought much of it. Last night he drove you back from the bar in his car and he told you he liked you. You laughed it off and pretended it didn't happen. As the night went on, Tony got more and more drunk and ended up falling asleep on your bed. When the others went home, you left Tony there and slept in the spare room. Tony is still asleep on your bed when you hear your husband's key in the door. You panic and you think he's going to jump to the wrong conclusion. He's always been the jealous type, and you're quickly trying to think on your feet. The improvisation starts after he's asked whose car it is for a second time, and you say it's a friend's from work. Your action is 'I do my best to explain'.
- Improvise the scene from this point and see where you end up.
- You will now improvise the scene, but without speech or gesture, just using rays.
- Think about communicating what you are thinking and feeling through rays rather than speech; you can still move around, but don't start gesturing.
- How did it feel to use just rays?
- Did you feel the improvisation could move on?
- Did you feel a bond and communication grow during the improvisation?

Notes for the student

This exercise shows how much of our communication is non-verbal and non-gestural. Much of what we say is through rays. The husband can look at his wife, think and communicate. The rays will then take it to her.

If you had a paint that could highlight rays and sprayed it inside a busy shopping centre, you would see a complete spider's web of lines at every angle, from person to person.

As you are improvising, allow your thoughts to flow and take over the space. When you go on to your next piece of text work, think about the presence of rays in communicating on stage.

Performance tip

Some actors can be very insular, with their characters never seeming to leave their bodies. Others actors seem to fill a theatre without seemingly doing anything. When people talk about presence on stage, they are often talking about the actor's ability to communicate their character to the whole audience while staying within the circumstances. Make sure you are allowing your character's objectives, actions and pictures from your imagination to fill the whole acting space and auditorium.

Student follow-on exercise: the nature of rays

Stanislavski said, 'It is as though our inner feelings and wishes give off rays, which pass through our eyes, our body and engulf other people in their stream.'[2] From the last exercise, did you experience what Stanislavski is talking about here? Think about the improvisation after you've finished it and see if you can recall how you communicated.

AS, A2, IB,
BTEC National.

32 THE NATURAL SILENCE

Student exercise: *The Apprentice*

AIM

To explore the silence on stage and how we communicate in that silence.

Three-person silence

- It's week six of The Apprentice, and you are project manager on this week's task. You are Simon, 34, and an estate agent from Slough.

This week was the shopping channel task, where you have to choose three objects to sell over the shopping channel. You chose a novelty alarm clock radio and a woman's designer jacket. Both sold fairly well. Sarah and Kerstin, who you have brought back into the boardroom with you, both chose a super speed remote control vacuum cleaner, which didn't sell at all. You lost the task and hold Sarah and Kerstin responsible for the failure. You have never really liked Kerstin and would like to see her fired this week. You tried to work with Kerstin on this task, but she never listened to a word you said and criticized you constantly. Sir Alan has just asked you to step outside while he confers with Margaret and Nick. You could cut the atmosphere with a knife. Your action is 'I prepare myself'. When you go back into the boardroom, you're going to 'go all out for' Kerstin to make sure she gets fired. There is no way you are being sent home this week.

- You are Kerstin, an ex-policewoman and marketing consultant from Warrington. You think you were 'right on the money' this task, and it's not your fault the vacuum cleaner didn't sell, even if you did choose it. You think Simon was a poor project manager; he never really led from the front and was too democratic. If there is one thing that you learned in the police – if you're in charge – you're in charge! Several times you told Simon that you should be selling the designer jacket, but he wouldn't listen. You think throughout the process you've sold well and shown that you should be the next apprentice. You're going to go back into that boardroom and tell Sir Alan how it really is – Simon doesn't know what he's doing. To prove you do, you are going to put yourself forward to be project manager on the next task. Your action is 'I intimidate'. You think there is no way you are going home this week and you can't believe Simon has lasted this long.

- You are Sarah; you're 26 and a media consultant from Newport, in Wales. You know that you didn't pick a very good product and that you didn't sell well. You have a feeling that Simon has a bit of a crush on you and guess that he's going to try to get Kerstin fired. To save yourself, all you have to do is suggest that you weren't really to blame for losing the task, and that, if you had a better product to sell, you would have easily won. You think Kerstin is too much trouble and you're going to happily let her talk herself into trouble, maybe even helping her along the way. Just in case, you have to make sure that Simon is on side, so you need to keep playing him along. If you've learned one lesson in business, it's that, to work with men, you need to keep them interested and thinking they might be in with a chance. Simon is no different; your action with him is 'I reassure – that you're here for him' and, with Kerstin, 'I gloat'.

- The natural silence will start as you leave the board room and go and sit down. You know you have at least two minutes before you'll be called back in. Allow your thoughts to communicate with each other. You know you can't say or do anything within the circumstances.

• Kerstin, you think you can psyche Simon out over the next two minutes, while Sarah, you are making sure Simon is 'on side'. Simon, you are thinking about what you will do when you get in to the boardroom.

• As the silence goes on, keep thinking within the context and adapting to what the others seem to be thinking. If you pick up on one of the others' rays, orientate and respond within the circumstances.

• Think about communicating through rays, but don't stop any physical impulses. Allow your body to be free to express your thoughts. Be careful not to start showing anything to the audience or each other. Trust your ability to communicate and be within the circumstances.

Notes for the student

This exercise is an example of the combination of the mind, body and spirit working in complete harmony. Afterwards, think about how close you got to experiencing the 'life of the human spirit of a role'.[3]

Taking away speech means you, as the actor, focus on other areas of communication that are just as powerful as the spoken word.

I always think some of the most beautiful moments on stage are during silences. The audience watches communication happening between the characters and actions working, and we get flashes of the characters' inner life.

For those of you who have watched *The Apprentice*, you'll understand the tension that could build within this silence when Sir Alan has asked the candidates to leave the room for a moment. It's fascinating to watch people who, on the surface, are trying to seem calm, while a torrent of emotions and actions are bubbling underneath.

Student follow-on exercise: watching Denzel

Watch a Denzel Washington film and observe how he communicates with both the other characters and the audience during silences. You look at him and you know what he is going to do next, how he feels about the situation he's in and the other people in the room. He doesn't show the audience what he is thinking, often it seems as if he is visibly doing nothing, but all the time he is experiencing his role, and his rays are picked up by us sitting at home or in the cinema. It's as if 5 per cent of him, as the actor, knows that the audience has to understand his character to enable them to understand the film. So, 95 per cent of his rays communicate within the circumstances as his character, with the remaining 5 per cent making sure the audience understands too. Within that 5 per cent, there is nothing shown to the audience, just thought, imagined and communicated.

Notes for the teacher

Natural silences work well as exercises in communication because they allow the student to focus on communicating, without always having to think of what to say next or what their next line is. Students can explore and experience in a relaxed way without thinking they have to perform.

Teacher extension exercise: communicating on film

Choose three actors and three actresses and pick one of the films you think were their best (this won't always be the biggest box office success).

Ask the students to watch the films or clips from the films and then come into class and feed back on how each actor and actress communicates. They can also comment on use of objectives, actions, imagination etc.

With YouTube, clips from films are easy to view. I'm sure the average student would know, much better than you or I, how to locate film clips easily on the Internet.

33 THE NATURAL SILENCE 2

AS, A2, IB, BTEC National.

Student exercise: Amsterdam

Three-person silence

- You are Fiona, aged 18, you've just finished your A levels and are travelling across Europe with your boyfriend, Den. You've been to all the major capitals and have come to Amsterdam, before heading to Paris and then home to Oxford. While you are in Amsterdam, you are keen on taking Den to see the Van Gogh gallery. Den moaned about going to the gallery and suggested a compromise. If he goes to the Van Gogh with you, you go the sex museum with him. Eventually you agree. You've spent a lovely morning at the Van Gogh and now are walking around the sex museum. For you, it's all a bit embarrassing, and Den's raucous laughter at some of the statues is making it all too much. You sit down on a bench, and Den goes off in search of coffee for both of you. You are staring at a statue and waiting for your coffee when someone sits down on the other side of the bench. You freeze; out of the corner of your eye you see it's your violin teacher. You think of getting up, but you don't want him to notice you. You go to get a book out of your bag and bury your head in it. Your action is 'I cringe', and the silence will start here.

- You are Carl, a 42-year-old musician, who lives in Oxford. You've been a musician for most of your life since leaving the Royal Academy of Music. You tour with different orchestras around Europe playing the violin. You have been in Amsterdam for four days, and this is your first day off. You spent the morning walking around the city when you stumbled across the sex museum. At first you walked past, but then you said to yourself, 'Well, I am in Amsterdam, I'll just pop in'. You've been walking around the museum and, being honest, you think it's all a bit tacky and dated. You sit on a bench and take out your guide to see where to go next. You look around the room and, to your horror, you see one of your violin students from back home in Oxford. You've taught Fiona for years, and she's a very promising violinist. You think of what you can say and decide to pretend you haven't seen her, and, hopefully, she hasn't seen you. You can't believe you were so stupid as to come in here and you start to get stressed when you think of the next time you arrive at Fiona's parent's house to give a lesson. Your action is 'I punish myself'.
- The natural silence will start with you both sitting at the bench; both of you don't want to get up as you'll be noticed, so you sit there and wait.

Notes for the student

Don't force the relationship or the communication; the temptation might be for Carl to show his stress rather than imagine it. Allow the silence to go on for a minute or two when Den comes back with the coffee. This will be your extension exercise, where the silence will turn into an improvisation.

Student extension exercise: Den enters

- Den, you arrive back with the coffee and walk over to Fiona. You've always been a bit cheeky and high-spirited, always looking to crack a joke and have some fun. While you were getting the coffees, you pretended to be American and seemed to get away with it. You're naturally a loud person, and the improvisation will start with you shouting to Fiona across the room in an American accent.
- Fiona and Carl, you both now realize that you cannot pretend you haven't seen each other, as the whole room has looked up at Den's noisy entrance.
- The improvisation starts from when Den shouts across to Fiona.

34 GUILTY OR INNOCENT?

Student exercise

AIM

To practise receiving rays and act upon them.

- Half of the class lines up and stands before the rest of the class. Each of them is given a piece of card. On all but one it says 'I'm innocent', and on one it says 'I'm guilty', with what they are guilty of written on the card (Figure 5.6).

Guilty

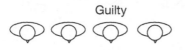

Figure 5.6
Guilty or innocent

- You can start simply and then get more adventurous; here are some examples:

  - I stole my friend's iPod.
  - I lied about doing my coursework.
  - I lied about my GCSEs to get into college.
  - I'm two-timing my girl/boyfriend.
  - I entered the country illegally.

- If you are innocent, just imagine you have done nothing wrong and communicate this to the students watching through rays, without doing or saying anything.
- The person who has the 'I'm guilty' card imagines themselves in the circumstances and thinks about what they have done wrong (Figure 5.7).
- Remember to relax and not to force or strain your imagination.
- The students observing then have to decide who is guilty. Don't shout out, but observe for about a minute and then each say who you think it is and why (Figure 5.8).

Figure 5.7
Who is guilty?

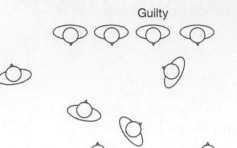

Figure 5.8
You're the guilty one

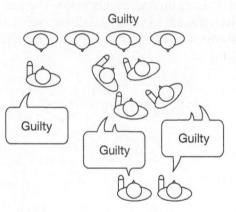

Notes for the student

If you are the guilty one, just imagine what has happened and create the circumstances actively in your imagination. Allow your thoughts to travel to the students watching and keep actively building imagined pictures as you go through the exercise.

If you are innocent, just think, 'I have done nothing wrong', and let the students watching know through radiation and rays.

Notes for the teacher

This exercise can be fascinating to watch. If the guilty student imagines the circumstances, allowing themselves to think actively, it soon becomes very obvious who the guilty one is. Students can start to use an action, 'I cover up', to hide their guilt, which can then be seen by the observers. This exercise, and the extension exercise, helps students to see that we communicate through pictures and images and by actively thinking within a circumstance. The audience can then form an idea of what a character is like.

Teacher extension exercise: good or evil

- Have the students line up in the same way and give them a card saying 'good' or 'evil' on it. If the student gets the 'good' card, they have to create a 'good' character. They put themselves in a circumstance with positive objective and action and allow the imagination to do the rest. For example an aid worker or a nurse.
- If they get the 'evil' card, they imagine they are an 'evil' character within a circumstance with an evil objective and action. Examples would be a serial killer or a murderer.
- Pick one student to walk along the row saying who is good and who is evil, deciding on their story as communicated to them by the actor.

35 AWARENESS

AS, A2, BTEC National, undergraduate.

Student exercise

AIM

To use the senses to help communicate with other actors in the space.

- One student stands at one side of the drama studio, with another student at the other side. Both students close their eyes and hold their arms out, with their palms facing the other person (Figure 5.9).

Figure 5.9
Starting the 'Awareness' exercise

Figure 5.10
Completing the 'Awareness' exercise

• Maintaining an awareness of the other person, both students, as quietly as they can, move towards each other, aiming to stop in front of each other with their hands together (Figures 5.10 and 5.11).

Notes for the student

You will need to use all your senses and communication skills to come together. Take your time; it's about you communicating with the other person, not seeing how quickly you can come together. Have a few goes, until you connect with the other person. After each go, think back to identify when and how the communication took place.

Group extension exercise: spatial awareness

• Find a space in the studio.
• Shut your eyes; give yourself ten seconds standing still to build up an awareness of everyone around you. Slowly start moving around the space, using your senses to make sure you don't collide with anyone.
• If you walk into someone, stop, refocus and slowly move on.
• Move your awareness around the room; try to picture in your mind's eye everyone else's positions around the room.

Figure 5.11
Practising the 'Awareness' exercise. Constance and Amber are just slightly off line here; ideally, your hands will meet perfectly, and it is worth practising until you get it spot on

Notes for the teacher

This exercise focusses the students on using their senses and sharpens their antennae. They have to calm themselves and really concentrate their attention in a direction they may not normally do. By heightening the senses, the student will start to experience the link between the mind and body.

36 RELATIONSHIPS

AS, A2, IB, BTEC National, undergraduate.

Student exercise: *The Seagull*

AIM

To analyse the text to start building a picture of the relationship between two characters.

- Read the extract from *The Seagull*. The action takes place towards the end of Act 4.
- With a partner, summarize what you think is happening.

- Research the basic plot of the play and write down the main events for each character for the play.
- Write down three things that Nina thinks about Konstantin and three things Konstantin thinks about Nina.
- Now look at the three things you have written down and ask yourself – if these are what the character thinks consciously, what do they think subconsciously? For example: what do you think Nina really thinks of Konstantin?
- Start to explore the subtext through the relationships by figuring out what they really think of each other, and not just what they are saying about each other.
- Decide on an action for your character in the scene and improvise the scene, thinking of the relationships you have decided upon.
- Sit down and discuss the improvisation with your partner. Did the relationships you decided on fit? If not, write down your improved relationships and improvise the scene again.
- Did it help the scene to have the relationships decided upon first?

Trepliov   Nina, I used to curse you: I hated you, I tore up your letters and photographs, but all the time I knew that I was bound to you heart and soul, and for ever! It's not in my power to stop loving you, Nina. Ever since I lost you, ever since I began to get my work published, my life's been intolerable. I'm wretched . . . I feel as if my youth has been suddenly torn away from me, as if I've been inhabiting this world for ninety years. I call out your name, I kiss the ground where you've walked; wherever I look I seem to see your face, that sweet smile that used to shine on me in the best years of my life . . .

Nina   [*bewildered*] Why does he talk like this, why does he talk like this?

Trepliov   I am lonely. I've no-one's love to warm me, I feel as cold as if I were in a cellar – and everything I write turns out lifeless and bitter and gloomy. Stay here, Nina, I entreat you, or let me come with you!

[*Nina quickly puts on her hat and cape*]

Trepliov   Nina, why – for Heaven's sake, Nina . . .

[*looks at her as she puts on her clothes*]

[*a pause*]

Nina   The horses are waiting for me at the gate. Don't see me off, I'll go by myself . . . [*tearfully*] Give me some water.

Trepliov   [*gives her water*] Where are you going now?

Nina   To the town. [*a pause*] Irena Nikolayevna's here, isn't she?

Trepliov   Yes . . . My uncle had an attack on Thursday, so we tele-graphed for her.

Nina   Why did you say you kissed the ground where I walked? Someone ought to kill me. [*droops over the table*] I am so tired. Oh I wish I could rest . . . just rest! [*raising her head*] I'm a seagull . . . No, that's not it. I'm an actress. Oh, well! [*she hears Arkadina and Trigorin laughing off-stage, listens, then runs to the door at left and looks through the keyhole*] So he is here too! . . . [*returning to Trepliov*] Oh, well! . . . Never mind . . . Yes . . . He didn't believe in the theatre, he was always laughing at my dreams, and so gradually I ceased to believe, too, and lost heart . . . And then I was so preoccupied with love and jealousy, and a constant fear for my baby . . . I became petty and common, when I acted I did it stupidly . . . I didn't know what to do with my hands or how to stand on stage, I couldn't control my voice . . . But you can't imagine what it feels like – when you know that you are acting abominably. I'm a seagull. No, that's not it again . . . Do you remember you shot a seagull? A man came along by chance, saw it and destroyed it, just to pass the time . . . A subject for a short story . . . That's not it. [*rubs her forehead*] What was I talking about? . . . Yes, about the stage. I'm not like that now . . . Now I am a real actress, I act with intense enjoyment, with enthusiasm; on the stage I am intoxicated and I feel that I am beautiful. But now, while I'm living here, I go for walks a lot . . . I keep walking and thinking . . . thinking and feeling that I am growing stronger in spirit with every day that passes . . . I think I now know, Kostia, that what matters is our work – whether you act on the stage or write stories – what really matters is not the fame, or glamour, not the things I used to dream about – but knowing how to endure things. How to bear one's cross and have faith. I have faith now and I'm not suffering quite so much, and when I think of my vocation I'm not afraid of life.

The Seagull, A. Chekhov, Penguin.[4]

Notes for the student

Relationships gel all the characters together on stage. Without them, all the characters would be in their own little worlds. By deciding upon the relationship your character has with another character, you will know exactly what you think of them and how to behave towards them. When you are improvising this scene, remind yourself of what you think about the other person as you look at them and allow your imagination to actively take it from there. This duologue/Nina's monologue and the one in the next exercise would work well as part of Edexcel's 'Text in performance' or the higher grades of the LAMDA acting syllabus.

Notes for the teacher

By deciding on the relationships, the students will know exactly what they think about everyone else on the stage. When visiting a school or college to work on a piece of text with students, I often notice the students have not thought through their relationships fully. The students have a vague idea of what they think, but nothing concrete. Taking five or ten minutes to sit down as a group and decide on all the relationships really helps the students connect together on stage. Delving into the subconscious with relationships can be a lot of fun, with students creating conflict and tension through the interaction of the characters.

AS, A2, IB,
BTEC National,
undergraduate.

37 RELATIONSHIPS 2

Student exercise: *Hysteria*

AIM

To use improvisation to analyse and build relationships.

- With a partner, read the extract from *Hysteria*, by Terry Johnson. The action takes place at the start of the play, in Sigmund Freud's study.
- With your partner, summarize what you think is happening, the main events.
- Divide the extract into bits and work out your actions.
- Improvise the scene, using the main events and actions to guide you.
- After the improvisation, evaluate what you have found out about the relationships. Did improvising the scene help to pin down what you think about the other characters? Give a label to the relationship that evolved when you improvised the scene.
- Think about your actions and decide on new ones if necessary.
- Improvise the scene again. Look again at your relationship with the other character and (if necessary) update the label you have given to the relationship.
- Re-read the extract and evaluate how the improvisations have helped you in working out the relationship between the two characters. Was

the second reading different from the first? Did the improvisations trigger your subconscious into working on the character?

- Do you find it easier to work out the relationship 'pencil in hand' discussing, or 'on your feet' improvising?

[*His eyes have closed.*

A pause, then a figure appears through the rain and stops outside the French windows. Jessica is sopping wet and initially appears waif-like. She wears a thin mackintosh. Her hair hangs dripping to her shoulders.

She taps on the glass. Freud opens his eyes. She taps again. He rises, disorientated, and discovers the source of the noise. She smiles.]

Freud   Go away. Go away. This is a private house, not Madame Tussauds. I admit I found it flattering when I arrived, this English passion for standing and staring, but I'd rather be melted down, thank you, than have any more thumbnails surreptitiously pressed into my flesh, so please . . . go away! Oh very well, stay where you are, catch your death for all I care. What do you want?

[*He goes to the intercom. She raps frantically. He doesn't press the buzzer. She speaks. We don't hear her through the glass.*]

Jessica   I have to speak to you.
Freud   What?
Jessica   I have to speak to you
Freud   I can't hear you. Go away.

[*Very matter-of-fact, she takes out a cut-throat razor and holds it to her wrist.*]

Jessica   I have to speak to you.

[*Freud looks away. Thinks. Then goes to the French windows and unlocks them. He steps back. She enters.*]

Freud   Stop there! Stop.

[*She stops, Closes the razor. Offers it to him. He takes it and secures it in a drawer.*]

Jessica   I wasn't sure you'd let me in.
Freud   You're sopping wet.
Jessica   It's raining.
Freud   That rug is from Persia.
Jessica   You told me to stop.
Freud   Get off the rug.

[*She steps forward.*]

Freud   No closer. Step sideways. To the left. Stand there.
Jessica   Here?
Freud   Good.
Jessica   Good.

Freud	How did you get in the garden?
Jessica	I climbed. Where the elm rests on the wall.
Freud	I'll have a tree surgeon to it first thing in the morning.
Jessica	Grazed my knee; look.
Freud	What are you, some sort of insomniac student?
Jessica	No.
Freud	You want me to read something you wrote?
Jessica	No.
Freud	Are you inebriated, irresponsible, rich? Is this a dare?
Jessica	No.
Freud	Do you know who I am?
Jessica	Oh yes.
Freud	Then what do you want?
Jessica	I don't know. I haven't yet decided.
Freud	Who are you?
Jessica	Don't you recognize me?
Freud	It feels as though I should.
Jessica	Yes, you should.
Freud	We've met?
Jessica	No, never.
Freud	Please. It's late. Who are you?
Jessica	I am your Anima, Professor Freud.
Freud	My what?
Jessica	It's a psychological term denoting the denied female element of the male psyche.
Freud	I know what it is.
Jessica	Denied but desired.
Freud	Damn nonsense, that's what it is. Did he send you?
Jessica	Who?
Freud	The Lunatic. Jung the crackpot, friend of the gods?
Jessica	No.
Freud	He did, didn't he? This is his feeble idea of a practical joke.
Jessica	No one sent me.

Hysteria, Terry Johnson, Methuen Royal Court
Writer Series.[5]

Notes for the student

By labelling the relationships, you have something to refer to in rehearsals and you always know what you think about the other people on stage. You can develop the relationship labels as much as you want; what is important is that you have thought about the relationship.

I included extracts from these two plays so you can practise analysing the relationships in a text and to introduce you to two wonderful plays. When I first read *Hysteria* I laughed out loud throughout and I wondered why no one had introduced me to the play earlier. So that's what I'm doing for you now!

While you are studying, it is important for you to read a variety of plays. You can then think how you would use the techniques in this book to help, if you were acting one of the characters. In the follow-on exercise, I have listed twelve plays for you to read, explore and enjoy.

Student follow-on exercise: plays to read

* The following plays are for you to read, think about and maybe use during your studies. They could be used to find a monologue or duologue, as part of a directorial analysis of an unseen text, or as inspiration for when presenting an extract from a play. This is by no means an exhaustive list, more of a starting point.

  * *Cat on a Hot Tin Roof*   Tennessee Williams
  * *Juno and the Paycock*   Sean O'Casey
  * *Marriage*   Nikolia Gogol
  * *Comedians*   Trevor Griffiths
  * *The Caretaker*   Harold Pinter
  * *American Buffalo*   David Mamet
  * *Red Roses and Petrol*   Joseph O'Connor
  * *Uncle Vanya*   Anton Chekhov
  * *Metamorphosis*   Steven Berkoff
  * *Jumpers*   Tom Stoppard
  * *The Assembley Women*   Aristophanes
  * *Private Lives*   Noel Coward

COMMUNICATION

Communication is the sending out and receiving of signals between two living beings.

Stanislavski described these signals as 'rays', an invisible current that flows between us all the time.

An actor on stage communicates with other actors on stage as his or her character and with the audience as the actor.

6 The super objective, through action and germ

through action
What the character does to achieve their super objective.

germ
The essence or seed of a character.

For you, the student, whether rehearsing a monologue or duologue or an extract from a play, or analysing a play from the point of view of the director, you will need a direction to go in, a path to follow. The super objective and **through action** will give you that. Stanislavski said the super objective and the through action had 'enormous practical significance',[1] and anything we do on stage that doesn't lead us in the direction of the super objective is unnecessary.

Stanislavski and his students had a super objective and through action for the play and a super objective and through action for each character. This meant they could sum up what the play was really about and the direction the play was going in, while each character had a direction and a sum of all the actions that drove them through the play.

If you are analysing a play from the director's perspective, sit together and decide on a working super objective for your play; this then gives you a direction to go in. If you are rehearsing a monologue or duologue, decide what you want as the character and start heading in that direction. If you are devising a piece of original theatre, give yourself a super objective at the start of the devising process. In that way, a confused or unfocussed piece can have a clear goal, and the through action can provide the means to achieving that goal.

In any given 'bit', we have an action driving us to achieve our objective. In a play, we have a through action driving us to achieve the super objective.

For me, when acting, it's the super objective and through action that give me direction and drive, while the **germ** grounds me in my before-time as the sum of my experiences to date. I couldn't imagine going on stage without them!

38 THE SUPER OBJECTIVE OF THE PLAY

AS, A2, IB,
BTEC National,
GCSE,
undergraduate.

Group exercise

AIM

To find the super objective of your chosen play and how the super objective can help you in the rehearsal process.

This exercise is related to a text and can be used with the text you are studying.

- Get into groups of four, with copies of the play you are studying.

  - You are going to work out the starter super objective for your play.
  - There is a list of questions that you need to answer. These will help you, as a group, to determine the super objective of your play.
  - Remember to work together, sharing ideas to build a picture of the playwright's intentions.

- Summarise the plot of the play in two or three lines.

  - Decide on the main themes, what you think the play is really about?
  - What do you think the playwright wanted the audience to think about the play?
  - Choose the main characters and start to work out their super objectives. Do they have anything in common?
  - Think about the social, political and historical context. What would it have been like to live at the time of the play? Does this affect the choice of super objective?
  - Now give a label to all your collected ideas and you have your starter super objective, and, as you work through the play, you can adapt and update your super objective.

- Now each group feeds back, so that you can all compare the choices you have made. You now have a direction to go in.

Remember, before the super objective of a play is chosen, the cast have no common goal; when rehearsing the play, they could all go in different directions (Figure 6.1).

   With a super objective for the play, the whole cast are going in the same direction, and the audience will see a clear direction from the actors on stage (Figure 6.2).

Figure 6.1
Possible paths in a play

Figure 6.2
The path of the super
objective

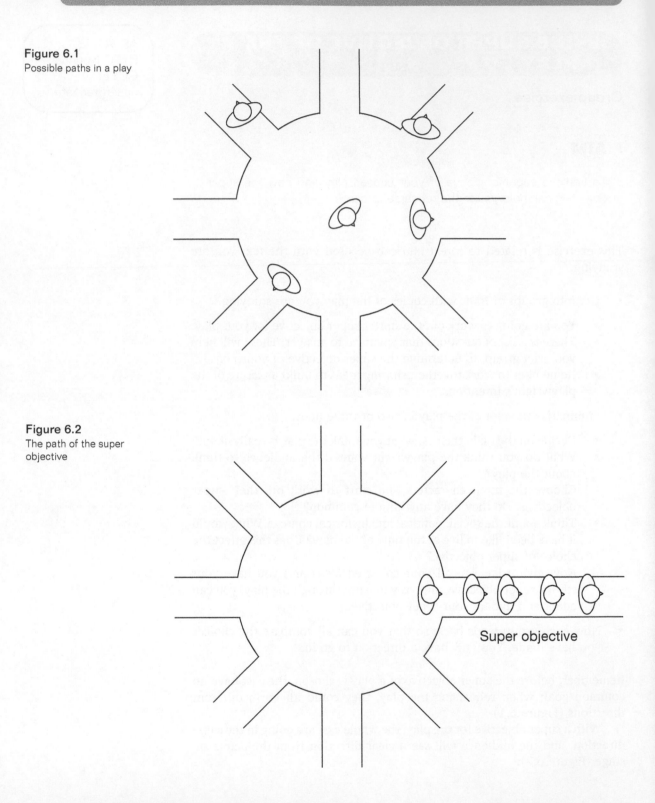

Super objective

Performance tip

The above exercise can be used whenever you are analysing a text. If you're looking at a play from the director's point of view, this exercise becomes even more important. The director, working with the cast, can make sure that everyone is going in the same direction and understands the play. When devising an original piece of theatre, think about the super objective early on and refer and update it as you go along. That way, you know your whole group is on the right track. It's better for you, as a group, to spend five minutes every few days on narrowing down the super objective, rather than leaving it to the dress rehearsal to find out that you're not all of the same mind.

Notes for the teacher

For the teacher, this exercise is a great way to observe how much of the play the students understand. By going through these questions, any grey areas or misunderstandings about the text will soon be ironed out. Use this exercise to get students to reflect on what the playwright really intended and start looking at the subtext of the play. Often, it's these discussions that really help the student to get inside the play. For BTEC National Diploma teachers, this task can be used in conjunction with examining the historical context of performance material.

Teacher extension task: researching the play

A working knowledge of the playwright is imperative when rehearsing a play. Send the students off to research the life of the playwright and find out the major events of their life. They can then use their findings when clarifying the super objective.

39 WHAT WE REALLY WANT

AS, A2, IB,
BTEC National,
GCSE,
undergraduate.

Teacher-led exercise

AIM

To understand what different people want in life, so you can transfer this understanding to the character's super objective.

Instructions for the teacher

- Sit the students in a semicircle and ask them what they want out of their lives, what they want to achieve and where they want to end up. I usually start off by going round the semicircle and, when a student says they 'don't know', I usually prompt them until they give an answer. Nine times out of ten, what they want will be positive – 'I want to have a good job' or 'I want to have a family' or, as one boy in a class full of girls said, 'I want to marry a Heat magazine girl' – I told him if he wants it enough I'm sure one day he'll get what he wants!

At this point, tell the class that what we want over the course of our lives is called the super objective.

- Now, split the group into three and ask them to look at the scenario in Table 6.1 and try to figure out the super objective of the character outlined.

Table 6.1 Billy's story

Billy grew up in North Wales and left school with four GCSEs; he then went on to college and studied business. Billy had always been a loner; his father died when he was young, and he spent a lot of time looking after his mother. His mother died when he was 22, and the house had to be sold, to pay off his mother's debts. Billy decided to move to London and rented a small bedsit in East London. He got a job in a small firm, working in sales. He was there for a couple of years, when, after a disagreement with his boss, he walked out on his job. After three months, he hadn't found another job, could no longer pay the rent and was out on the street. He lived in a couple of hostels, but didn't like living in a dormitory.

Billy ended up living under Waterloo Bridge and has done for the last ten years.

- Ask the class why they think Billy ended up on the streets and what they think he wanted. Often, students will say that 'he wants to get money' or 'he wants to find a job'.

It's at this point that I say, if he wanted to get money, he would logically have done something to get it. Therefore, it's our job as actors to figure out what he really wanted. To do this, we need to delve into the subconscious.

- Ask the students what they think he wants subconsciously – i.e. what thoughts he has that he can't necessarily see, but are the ones driving his life. This is usually where students will say something like, 'maybe he wants to be alone'. I often say that we are looking for a starter super objective and one that we can develop and revise as we work on our character. I offer another suggestion, that maybe Billy 'wants to have no responsibilities'. He wants to have no bills, no rent and no job to worry about, but just to go through life with no worries, apart from getting food and where he will sleep that night.

Notes for the teacher

I use the example of Billy to show the student that, when looking for the super objective, we need to dig deep to work out what they really want.

In every workshop I run, I do this type of exercise early on, and it always gets the students thinking and it starts to shift their focus to the subtext and what characters really want. I have yet to come across a student who doesn't understand, in principle, the idea of the subconscious want or desire present in us all. When working out a character's super objective, it's amazing how quickly students tap into the subconscious. When examining Nora in A Doll's House, *students start with 'Nora wants to do her best for the family', but, before long, students have already reached 'Nora wants to make Torvald suffer to exact revenge for years of being patronised'.*

Student follow-on exercise: into the subconscious

*   Look at the five professions listed in Table 6.2. For each profession, work out a super objective that best fits that profession. Imagine a character; think about where he/she might live; do they have a family? Do they own a house? Did they go to university?
*   Write down your super objective and then ask yourself – if this is a conscious super objective, what would the subconscious super objective be?
*   With a partner, compare notes and explain your choices.
*   Now look at the list in Table 6.3; this time, there is an adjective to describe the character. In what way does this change the super objective?

We can see that even having an adjective to describe the character makes it easier to narrow down the super objective. You can imagine, as you go through the process of finding out about your character's past, the giving of a label makes the super objective become clearer and clearer. That's why Stanislavski and his actors always had a starter super objective and updated it throughout the rehearsal process.

Table 6.2
Characters

Baker
Firefighter
Politician
Las Vegas showgirl
New aircraft test pilot

Table 6.3
Describing the characters

Award-winning baker
Conscientious firefighter
Corrupt politician
Frustrated Las Vegas showgirl
Cautious new aircraft test pilot

AS, A2, IB,
BTEC National,
GCSE.

40 THE CHARACTER'S THROUGH ACTION

AIM

To work out the through action of a character.

Student individual exercise

- Take a character from a play you are studying.
- Go through the play and, for each bit, write down the main action your character has in that bit.
- Write all the actions down in a list.
- Looking over your list, you should have a clear idea of the highs and lows of the journey of your character.
- Your through action will be the sum of all the actions of your character in the play, driving you towards the end of the play and to achieve your super objective.
- You can always refer to the actions list on page 26 for help on deciding your through action.

Notes for the student

The through action will help you to maintain your focus through a performance. By deciding on your through action, you have a path to follow that truly reflects the changes in your character's thinking and what they are doing. By going through this process, you may discover things you never realized about your character. This will help you build and create a character for a performance. Just remember, if we have an action to achieve an objective over a bit, we have a through action to achieve a super objective over a play.

AS, A2, IB,
BTEC National,
GCSE,
undergraduate.

41 THE GERM OF MY CHARACTER

Group exercise

AIM

To choose the germ or seed of the character around which the character can start to grow.

Now you are armed with the super objective, you have a clear impression of the direction your character is going in; the germ now gives you a clear idea of what you, the character, are like. This exercise allows you, early on, to label what you are like as the character and use this as the foundation around which you build your character.

- In your group, choose one name from each of the following three groups and start to decide on a germ for that character. The germ will be their essence – what they are like deep down. The germ starts with 'I'm', as in 'I'm capable'. You can refer to Table 6.4 for examples of a germ. The germ can work on different levels; you may start with a conscious germ and then work towards a more subconscious one.

  Macbeth
  Juliet
  Hamlet

  Winston Churchill
  Margaret Thatcher
  Tony Blair

  David Beckham
  Kelly Holmes
  Jonny Wilkinson

- Then, think about a play you have been studying recently and work out the germ for the main character. The choice you make for the germ will send your character down a particular path, so weigh up all the options carefully. For example, for Macbeth, you could choose 'I'm powerful', but, as you delve into Macbeth's subconscious, you might choose 'I'm trapped' or 'I'm frightened'. These more subconscious germs would bring in the relationship with Lady Macbeth and the fear simmering under the surface that can be seen in Macbeth's soliloquies.

Table 6.4 Examples of the germ of a character

I'm capable	I'm innocent	I'm a genius	I'm lonely	I'm a victim	I'm cocky
I'm devious	I'm a winner	I'm irritating	I'm brave	I'm selfish	I'm lost
I'm a cheeky little boy	I'm superior	I'm inferior	I'm lazy	I'm conscientious	I'm cheeky
I'm a loser	I'm desirable	I'm a joker	I'm special	I'm damaged	I'm lucky
I'm confused	I'm a hero	I'm misunderstood	I'm a witch	I'm frightened	I'm unloved
I'm a reject	I'm weak	I'm strong	I'm vicious	I'm trapped	

Note for the student

Three questions I often ask a student are: What are you like? What do you want and how are you going to achieve it? The answers are your germ, super objective and through action. By deciding these early on in rehearsal, you can clearly map out where your character is going and what they are like.

I have an ex student who, when working on a character, will email me with a starter super objective, through action and germ. I'll then email her back with what I think, and we'll go from there. Stanislavski, by giving us labels, made our job easier to do. We can pin down what the character is thinking and doing and make sure our character's journey is logical within the circumstances.

Notes for the teacher

Often in workshops, I'll stop a student and say, 'what's your character like?' On many occasions, the student will have the 'I'd never thought of it like that' look. The germ gives the student a clear definition of their character – something to hold on to as they work and build. I always introduce the germ early on when rehearsing, so I know the student has time to think about their character. I often use the metaphor of a trifle, with each layer of a character having a different quality. With the germ, the student will start with the top layer, and I'll be guiding them down to the fruity bits at the bottom. The journey they go on, as they work through these layers, means they really get under the skin of their character. The nature of your group determines how far you go – for a GCSE class, you may only want to dip just under the surface, whereas, with your IB or A2 students exploring a set text, you may want them to explore the full depths of the character. Some of my favourite moments in a workshop are when a student will turn round and say, 'I can't believe Hedda, she's such a devious bitch', and I'll say, 'looks like you have the startings of a germ!'

inner monologue
The thoughts going through our character's mind.

AS, A2, IB, BTEC National, GCSE.

AIM

To work out the character's inner monologue from a piece of text.

42 THE INNER MONOLOGUE

Student exercise

- Look at the two monologues from *Macbeth*. Work out the **inner monologue** for each character – what is going through their mind while they are saying these words.
- Remember that the inner monologue reflects the character's real thoughts and so is often different from what is spoken. We know from later events that Lady Macbeth isn't able to kill Duncan, and her evil deeds eventually drive her insane. With this in mind, her inner monologue may be less convincing than her spoken words.

Lady Macbeth:

The raven himself is hoarse
That croaks the fatal entrance of Duncan
Under my battlements. Come, you spirits
That tend on mortal thoughts, unsex me here
And fill me, from the crown to the toe, top-full
Of direst cruelty! Make thick my blood,
Stop up the access and passage to remorse,
That no compunctious visitings of nature
Shake my fell purpose nor keep peace between
The effect and it! Come to my woman's breasts,
And take my milk for gall, you murdering ministers,
Wherever in your sightless substances
You wait on nature's mischief! Come, thick night,
And pall thee in the dunnest smoke of hell,
That my keen knife see not the wound it makes,
Nor heaven peep through the blanket of the dark
To cry, 'Hold, hold!'

Macbeth, Act 1, Scene 5.[2]

Macbeth:

She should have died hereafter;
There would have been a time for such a word.
Tomorrow, and tomorrow, and tomorrow
Creeps in this petty pace from day to day
To the last syllable of recorded time;
And all our yesterdays have lighted fools
The way to dusty death. Out, out, brief candle!
Life's but a walking shadow, a poor player
That struts and frets his hour upon the stage
And then is heard no more. It is a tale
Told by an idiot, full of sound and fury,
Signifying nothing.

Macbeth, Act 5, Scene 5.[3]

Notes for the student

By writing down your inner monologue, you have something to refer to so that you remember what your character is thinking during a particular bit of the play. The inner monologue runs alongside the objective and action.

Don't think you have to write a huge amount; just jot down the thoughts of the character so you can refer to them later.

SUPER OBJECTIVE, THROUGH ACTION AND GERM

You can have a super objective for the play and a super objective for the character.

The super objective is the root of the play, the sum of all the objectives of the characters; it's what the play is really about.

For a character, the super objective is what they want over the course of the play.

The character's through action is what the character does to achieve the super objective. This is the sum of all their actions in the play. The through action drives a character to achieve their super objective.

Each character has a germ, the essence or seed of their character.

7 Events

The large majority of plays you will come in contact with are event driven. An event can be something that others do or something you think. As an actor, you need to be able to act an event truthfully.

Often, when working with a piece of text, it is the unexpected events that cause students the problems. For example, when, in *A View from the Bridge*, Eddie pulls a knife on Marco, all the others on stage have an event. It is the event of Eddie pulling the knife that is often shown through facial expression rather than allowed to manifest through a moment of orientation and a change in the objective and action. The student knows they have to 'react' and, often unsure how to do this, they decide on a facial expression.

When there is an event, such as someone pulling a knife, anyone watching will experience what Stanislavski called a moment of orientation. It always takes us a moment to register what has happened, what we feel about it and what we are going to do about it. If we don't have this moment on stage, our acting can look fake and rushed. We all have this moment of orientation to every event that happens. It's this moment of orientation that the armed forces work very hard on reducing. If, tomorrow, you or I were put in a combat situation, the continual barrage of events would mean we orientate rather than act on these events. A trained, experienced soldier will have been conditioned to orientate less and act quicker. It's that shorter moment of orientation that will save their lives!

This chapter will introduce you to exercises that will help you to act an event in the play believably and within the circumstances. We have all seen 'bad horror acting', where actors try to show their horror at a series of events. These exercises are about giving you the tools to walk through an event, so that it is believed by the audience as logical within the circumstances of the play.

AS, A2, IB,
BTEC National,
GCSE.

43 THE UNEXPECTED EVENT

Teacher-led exercise

AIM

To understand how to act an unexpected event within a set of given circumstances.

Two-person improvisation

- The first scenario is based in a doctor's surgery, with one student playing the doctor, and the other student coming in for a health check.

  - Student 1, you are a doctor, it's Friday afternoon, and you have one patient left; you have recently joined a tennis club and are booked in to have a couple of sets with a colleague after work. The last patient of the day is booked in to have a health check. Your objective is 'I want it over and done with so I can get on court quicker', and your action is 'I do my duty'.

  - Student 2, you have recently got a new job in a bank that, as part of your salary package, offers private health care. Your new employers have asked you to get a health check with your doctor before you sign up with the private health care company. You have booked this afternoon off and popped home first to get changed before you walked down to the doctor's. Your objective is 'I want to find out if I'm fit and healthy', and your action is 'I bide my time' while you wait to hear what the doctor will say.

  - The improvisation starts when the patient walks in. Halfway through the improvisation, your teacher will say 'TAP'. This is for student 2; student 1: imagine you have not heard it. When you hear the word 'TAP', imagine that, before you left the house, you had a quick wash and you think you have left the tap running. You start to imagine the water flooding the bathroom and going through the ceiling into the lounge below. Your event is thinking you may have left the tap on.

  - Remember, you are in a social situation, and so you probably cannot just run out of the surgery.

  - Improvise the scene with the objective and action and, when the event happens, see what happens to the improvisation.

- For the audience: you need to observe and then comment on whether you think student 2 had an event, and, if so, whether it seemed to come from the circumstances or appeared shown or fake.

Notes for the teacher

This exercise is great for students to experience an event and to see how they should act the event. Usually, on the first go, students will show the event to the audience and it will not be believable. This is where you can tell students that they do not need to show the event, but rather imagine it actively, as if it were happening, and then the audience will believe it. After a few goes, the group will start to see that having an unexpected event is more to do with imagining it than showing it.

You can ask the students if they think their behaviour fitted the given circumstances and their character. Students will sometimes say, 'if that was me I'd have run out', to which I reply that it's not them, it is them playing a professional man/woman with a clear objective to get a health check done. This is also a good time to decide if they had the objective and action originally decided upon.

This exercise highlights the difference between imagining an event, allowing it to manifest physically, and showing an event through facial expression. When we have an event, it is followed by a moment of orientation that will lead into a new action and objective. An example of the process is shown in Figure 7.1.

I want to find out	Moment of orientation	I want to retrace my steps
$\Rightarrow$ **TAP** $\Rightarrow$	$\Rightarrow$	
I bide my time	I orientate	I panic

Figure 7.1
The TAP event

44 THE INTERVIEW

AS, A2, IB, BTEC National, GCSE.

Teacher-led exercise

- Student 1, you work in advertising as a creative manager, which means you are in charge of a team that comes up with ideas for adverts, jingles, billboard campaigns, magazine adverts etc. You are always on the lookout for sharp minds with creative ideas. Today, you are interviewing graduates for a position in your team. You have asked candidates to prepare ideas on an advert for Pepsi. Your objective is 'I want to find out if they are any good' and action 'I test'.

- Student 2, you have recently graduated from Oxford with a first in literature. You have always been fascinated by advertising; today's interview is a real opportunity to work with the best there is. You arrived early and have your ideas on Pepsi planned. You are going to suggest an ad campaign focussing on the world's most famous people in their daily lives. Towards the end of the advert, we see that Pepsi plays a part. For example, Tom Cruise shopping, shot in a documentary style, walking home from the shops, sits on the couch, picks up a script to read, reaches into the bag, takes out a Pepsi and starts to drink. Your objective is 'I want to do my best in the interview' and action 'I impress'.
- The improvisation starts with the interviewee entering the room. Halfway through the improvisation, your teacher will say 'IRON'. Student 2, you now think that you have left the iron on. You were ironing your top this morning and you think that you forgot to switch the iron off. The ironing board is by the window, and you left the top window open, which could blow your curtains on to the iron, and they could catch fire. You start to imagine your curtains on fire and the whole flat burning down. But remember, you are in the interview of a lifetime!

Notes for the teacher

This event often leads to an internal struggle for the candidate, with them thinking about the iron while trying to seem calm in the interview. Before 'IRON', the interviewee will often be speaking enthusiastically about Pepsi and, with the event, they start to hesitate and lose their train of thought. One student doing this exercise visibly blushed, and you could see the muscles of her face tighten. This physical reaction came from imagining the event and was believable to the audience. It's a good idea to highlight where there is a facial expression or movement that comes directly from the event and the circumstances.

Student follow-on exercise: analysing an event

- Figure 7.2 is a diagram taken from the 'Unexpected event' exercise, to use as an example for this exercise. It follows the objective and action to the event, then the moment of orientation and the new objective and action. It then has the same sequence as an inner monologue – what the characters' thoughts are as they think them.
- For the IRON improvisation, use Figure 7.3. Work out what your new objective and action were after the event and complete the inner monologue section to determine how your thinking changed. You can use the actions list in Chapter 2 to help.

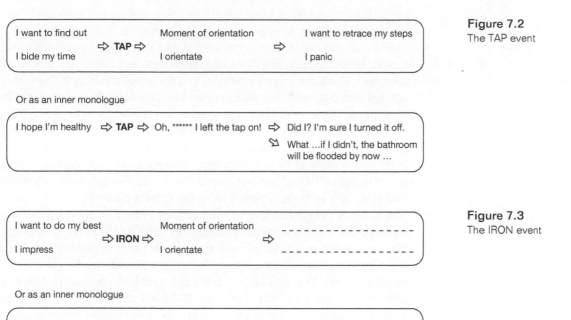

Figure 7.2
The TAP event

Figure 7.3
The IRON event

- Look back over the exercise and answer these questions:
  - Were there any physical changes when you had the event?
  - Were they linked to the psychological changes?
  - How did it feel to experience the event?
  - How did the event trigger off a new set of actions and objectives?

45 *BLUE PETER*

AS, A2, IB,
BTEC National,
GCSE.

Teacher-led exercise

- Student 1, you are a *Blue Peter* presenter, you have been with *Blue Peter* for over a year and have been very successful and popular. You recently had a meeting with your agent and you said you want to work for a prime-time show. Your agent agreed and told you he is going to start making calls, but first he needs a recent interview to show people. You tell him you have got an interview coming up in a school and that you'll make sure it is a good one. *Blue Peter* is sending you to a school in Surrey that has started a massive, county-wide recycling project. It was the brainchild of one Year 10 student who you are set to interview. Your objective is 'I want to impress', and your action is 'I shine'.

- Student 2, you are in Year 10 at school and recently, as part of a PSHE lesson, looked at recycling. You suggested that, as a form, you should all start recycling more conscientiously. You then took the idea to the school council and proposed that all forms and all years should be recycling. In a couple of weeks, you have managed to get the whole school recycling and have even given a talk to the nearest school. Now, your scheme is going to be adopted across the county. Yesterday you were told that *Blue Peter* was coming in to interview you. You spent all last night worrying about being on TV and looking stupid. Your objective is 'I want to survive and look OK', with the action 'I keep my fingers crossed'.
- The show is being shot live as part of *Blue Peter Live* month; halfway through the interview, your teacher will say 'COOKER'. At this point, the *Blue Peter* presenter thinks they have left the cooker on. This morning, you were making scrambled eggs when the studio car arrived to pick you up. You quickly ate the eggs, grabbed your notes and bag and went to the car. You think you have left the cooker on and you begin to imagine the frying pan heating up and eventually catching fire and your whole kitchen full of flames.
- Remember, this is going out live, so, even though you may be internally panicking, you will need to try to cover up the event.
- After the improvisation, look back and see how the event changed the way you were presenting and what you were thinking.

46 KNOCK AT THE DOOR

Student exercise

AS, A2, BTEC National, GCSE, undergraduate.

AIM

To practise expected and unexpected events in differing circumstances.

- In Table 7.1 there is a list of five characters in five different situations.
- Student 1, choose a character and situation from Table 7.1 and go out of the room.
- Student 1 then knocks at the door as that character.
- Student 2 answers the door and improvises responding to the person at the door.

- When student 2 opens the door, you will have been expecting that person to come. This means you have a good idea of what will happen and what to expect.
- Before you hear the knock, imagine you are at home, the time of day and that you are waiting for the person to arrive (Figure 7.4).
- Decide on your objective and action and then allow the improvisation to take its course.

Table 7.1
Characters and situations

A Parcel Force driver coming to deliver a parcel from America

A plumber coming to have a look at your boiler

The landlord coming round to check the washing machine

A friend who said she was popping round to watch TV

Your flatmate, who has lost their keys again and is coming back from work

Figure 7.4
Knock at the door

- Now student 2 will be at home, about to watch a film, when you hear a knock at the door; you are not expecting anyone and wonder who it is (Figure 7.5). You go to the door and open it.

Figure 7.5
Unexpected knock at the door

- Your objective is 'I want to find out who it is', and your action is 'I orientate'. Allow the event of the person at the door and what they have to say to change your objective and action after the moment of orientation.
- In Table 7.2, there is a further list of characters and situations for student 1 to use.
- If you are student 2 answering the door, make sure you don't know what character student 1 will be playing.

Table 7.2 Characters and situations 2

A policeman wanting to question you about an incident that occurred late last night

A neighbour who has lost their dog

A canvasser from the Labour Party

An official from the local council who has been called to your address after reports of continual loud music

A Tarzan-a-Gram who has been booked for a hen night

Notes for the student

Think about the difference between an expected event and one that is unexpected. When we are expecting something, we have an objective and action that go in the direction of that event. For example, if it's the first day of a new job, my event could be meeting the other cast and crew. My objective and action will be what I want to achieve when I meet them. But, if, on the way to the job, I hear some tragic news, this unexpected event will mean I have a new objective and action relating to the new event, and the old event will no longer seem as important.

Observe how you anticipate events and react to unexpected events. Within these improvisations, you may have felt the temptation to show your event or show your surprise/shock. If this temptation arises, just relax and allow your imagination to do the work.

You may, in the past, have been used to using facial expression to tell the audience what you are thinking. Stanislavski said, 'you can't teach facial expression, as what you get from that is face pulling. Facial expression happens of itself, naturally, through intuition or inner experiencing.'[1]

What Stanislavski is saying is, if you pull a face to let the audience know you're shocked, the audience will just think, 'Oh they're pulling a face'. If you allow your imagination and moment of orientation, within a given circumstance, to manifest in your face, then the audience will believe in your performance.

Notes for the teacher

You can use this exercise to highlight how students use facial expression when having events. I know, especially at GCSE, with the use of facial expression being assessed, students are aware of the impact of facial expression. Students often can stylize a facial expression, but cannot act it truthfully. During this exercise, you can point out when you think they are face pulling and when the expression comes from 'inner experiencing'.

Teacher extension exercise: the meeting

- *Ask a student to wait outside the room and, while they are out of earshot, decide on the event that will greet them when they come back in.*
- *For example, the student outside opens the door and walks in, and everyone starts clapping and goes up and shakes hands, congratulating the student.*
- *Then ask the same student to go outside, and you'll do exactly the same again, and ask the student to have the event without showing or forcing, but orientating and then deciding on a new objective and action.*

EVENTS

An event is something that happens that affects what we are thinking and doing.

As an actor, you can have an expected event, one that you know is going to happen, and an unexpected event, one that you do not know will happen.

Stanislavski and his actors would decide on the main event (the main thing that had happened) for a bit of the text, when working on a play.

8 Tempo-rhythm, voice and movement

tempo-rhythm
Our pace, both mental and physical, the pace of everything around us and everything we do.

We all have a **tempo-rhythm**. Our tempo-rhythm depends on events, our mood and our actions. Our tempo-rhythm is a reflection of our actions and objectives. We can be perfectly still, yet have a fast tempo-rhythm. I often ask students to tap out the tempo-rhythm of their character in a scene or bit of the play. This helps you to understand the objective and action and therefore the pace of the scene.

Stanislavski said, 'where there is *life* there is *action*, and where there is *action* there is *movement*, and where there is *movement* there is *tempo*, and where there is *tempo* there is *rhythm*.'[1]

The actor's voice and body are important instruments of communication. If the actor's voice cannot be heard, or his movements are wooden and unnatural, the majority of the other areas of the system will be lost on the audience. As one director I worked with put it during rehearsals, 'you might be the best actor in the world but if the audience can't hear you, you might as well be the worst.'

As students of drama, it is your job to work on your voice and movement skills so you can embody your character on stage. We have all seen actors who 'head act' and don't allow the thoughts and actions of the character to manifest in their movement, or actors whose voices seem disconnected from their character.

While in Moscow, I attended a gymnastics class at one of the drama schools. At the time, I was in my third year of drama school, with two years of gymnastics/acrobatics under my belt; I thought I had reached a good standard and was eager to compare. The level of gymnastics I saw was amazing, and all on a hard wooden floor. I sat through the class and, at the end, turned to the girl next to me and asked if this was the gymnastics team. She shook her head and said they were just normal, first-year, acting students. These students were all dedicated to producing a finely tuned physicality to embody their character. Exactly what Stanislavski would have wanted from his students eighty years earlier.

This chapter will outline exercises in tempo-rhythm and some simple voice and movement exercises for you to practise. I recommend that, together with yoga, you attend a dance/gymnastics class to work on improving your posture and alignment, and a singing class to begin your voice work. Those of you thinking of auditioning for drama school will find these classes invaluable and a lot of fun! You will probably be auditioning alongside students who have danced since they were five or had regular singing lessons, so it's best to start thinking about those skills now, while you have time to work on them.

For students studying for the BTEC National qualification, this chapter, combined with the exercises in free body and communication, will help fulfil the syllabus criteria for physical preparation, warm-ups, relaxation exercises, vocal exercises and communication and collaborative skills.

47 TEMPO-RHYTHM

AS, A2, IB,
BTEC National,
undergraduate.

Student exercise

AIM

To experience the inner and outer tempo-rhythm in us and everything around us.

- Sit on a chair and pull yourself up by the strings.
- Tap out the tempo-rhythm for Covent Garden on a Friday night. Imagine you are standing in the middle of Covent Garden; you can hear the throng of people, the sounds of traffic, music from bars and the energy of people on a night out. When you have the impression, start to tap it out.
- Now tap a Sunday afternoon in the country. Imagine the fields, trees, birds flying overhead and tap the tempo-rhythm. Compare the tempo-rhythm with Covent Garden on a Friday night.
- Clap the tempo-rhythm of a boxer fighting in the ring and slowly move to a girl reading in a library. Remember to fill your head with the impression of the fight or the library. Use the skills you learned with the visualization exercise (Chapter 3) to feed into clapping out the tempo-rhythm.
- Tap or clap anger: create a circumstance when you would be angry and tap or clap. Then imagine you are on your own, and have been for a long time, and tap or clap that tempo-rhythm.
- Imagine you are standing by river rapids; clap or tap out the tempo-rhythm and then change to a garden pond; move from the pond to the rapids, watching for the change in tempo-rhythm as you go.

Notes for the student

As you start to identify the tempo-rhythm in things around you, observe how they change. Tap or clap out the tempo-rhythm and start to notice the changes. For example, the boxer's tempo-rhythm would change continually during the fight. You can start to register a physical blow or a psychological event with the tapping of the tempo-rhythm.

Student follow-on exercise: clap or tap

Over the next few days, clap or tap the tempo-rhythm of objects and people around you. Clap the tempo-rhythm of an old woman shopping, and then a young guy driving, and compare them.

Look for changes in your own tempo-rhythm and try to catch yourself unawares; when you are in the middle of something, think 'what is my tempo-rhythm?' and tap it out. Then, a couple of hours later, do the same and compare the different tempo-rhythms. If you have a big event, observe your tempo-rhythm and tap or clap it out. By practising tapping or clapping out the tempo-rhythm, you are creating a tempo-rhythm register that you can then use with a character, objective, action, emotion and a bit of the play.

AS, A2, IB,
BTEC National,
undergraduate.

48 TEMPO-RHYTHM AND THE CHARACTER

AIM

To use tempo-rhythm with a character and a bit of the play.

Student exercise

* Work through each character and situation (Table 8.1) and clap or tap out their tempo-rhythm.
* Remember to imagine actively the circumstances and, once you have an impression of the character, clap or tap.
* Then choose a character from Table 8.2, with an adjective relating to their situation, and clap or tap the tempo-rhythm.

Table 8.1 Character tempo-rhythm

An astronaut about to walk in space
An actor about to receive an Oscar
A gardener pruning the roses
A taxi driver waiting at the rank
A beautician about to give a film star a facial

Table 8.2 Character tempo-rhythm 2

A despairing student having failed her A levels

A jubilant businessman signing a million-dollar deal

A distraught daughter who has lost a parent

A joyous father holding his newly born son

A shocked swimmer who's just been saved by a lifeguard

Student extension task: clapping a character

* Choose a character from the play you are studying and tap or clap their tempo-rhythm.
* Then match up their tempo-rhythm with the character's super objective, through action and germ.
* Choose a bit of the play and clap or tap the tempo-rhythm of your character in that bit. Use this to help work out the objective and action for your character in that bit.

Notes for the student

You can use tempo-rhythm with every part of the system you have learned so far. If you are finding it hard to work out an objective or action, clap the tempo-rhythm, and that will help guide you. After you have played a scene, you can clap the tempo-rhythm you wanted to have and compare it with the tempo-rhythm you actually had. When directing others, you can always say, 'I thought in this scene your tempo-rhythm was more . . .', and tap it out for them, so that the actor can understand what you want.

49 RESONATORS

AS, A2, IB,
BTEC National,
GCSE, KS3.

Student exercise

AIM

To locate and harness resonators in the upper body and head.

* Stand in a space in the studio and, with your mouth shut, gently start to hum.

- Imagine filling your head with the humming sound and feel the vibrations around your head.
- Move the humming sound to the end of your nose, so you can feel the vibrations. Imagine that you are sending the vibration to the end of your nose.
- Move your head forward and drop your chin, continuing to hum.
- Gently move the humming to the back of your head; try to fill all the different parts of the back of your head with the hum.
- Move the humming to the throat and imagine the sound filling your neck. Now move the hum around your head and throat.
- Gently start to tap your chest with your fingers, moving the sound to your chest.
- Open your mouth to a yawning position and hum for five seconds.
- Start to introduce a range of notes into the hum and move the hum around your head, throat and chest.

Notes for the student

This exercise will help you to locate the natural resonators you can use to support your voice. Do not forget to breathe as you do this exercise; move on to a different resonator when you need to take a new breath. Explore the sound and the effect it has as it travels around your head. Observe the vibrations and which ones seem stronger than others. By locating and working on the resonators, you will start to produce a clearer sound when you move from humming to speech. Watch for any changes in your speech after humming and locating the resonators in your head and upper body.

Notes for the teacher

You can do this exercise as part of a vocal warm-up and you can extend the exercise by adding sound after a few seconds' humming, so that the student can see the clarity of the sound.

AS, A2, IB,
BTEC National,
GCSE, KS3.

50 FILLING THE ROOM

Student exercise

AIM

To work on projection and extending the vocal quality.

- In pairs, stand opposite each other at one end of the drama studio. Student A (with back to the wall) is going to be the one to recite a nursery rhyme.
- Student B will slowly walk back from student A until they are at the opposite end of the studio (Figure 8.1).

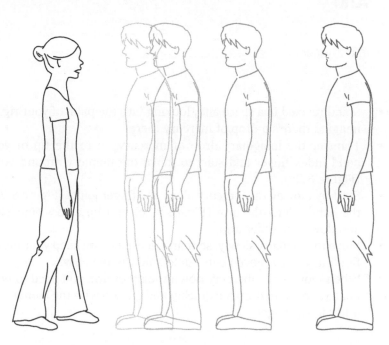

Figure 8.1
Filling the room

- Student A starts whispering and, as student B walks back, student A must increase the volume and project their voice to reach student B.
- Remember not to shout, and increase the volume of your voice consistently. Imagine your voice connecting with your resonators.
- When student B is at the far end of the studio, imagine a target over their head that your voice needs to penetrate. Imagine filling the room with your voice, all the time maintaining your breathing and without straining your voice.
- Swap around, so that student A now walks up to where student B is standing and slowly starts to walk backwards.

Notes for the student

Try to increase your voice at a steady rate and be careful not to strain, as you have to hit the target at the end. Start to think about how your breath connects with your diaphragm as you inhale and exhale.

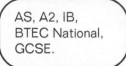

AS, A2, IB,
BTEC National,
GCSE.

51 THE FLEXIBILITY OF MOVEMENT

Student exercise

AIM

To focus attention on the physical self and work on greater flexibility in movement.

- Stand relaxed in a space and, looking into the palm of your right hand, imagine there's a drop of mercury there.
- Transfer the imaginary drop of mercury on to the tip of your left-hand index finger and start to move the mercury around your body (Figure 8.2a).
- Start by moving the mercury along the finger joints (Figure 8.2b), over the hand, along the arm (Figure 8.2c) and up across your shoulders and down the other arm.
- Move the mercury slowly, so that it doesn't drop; keep your movements fluid: any jerky movements could spill the mercury.
- When moving the mercury down the other arm you need to be careful not to allow it to drop too quickly and end up with the mercury on your other index finger.

Figure 8.2a
Moving mercury

Figure 8.2b
Moving mercury along the arm

Figure 8.2c
Moving mercury along
the arm

- Now imagine the mercury is sitting on the crown of your head and slowly passing down your head, over your neck and along your spine.
- Imagine the mercury passing down one leg and up again and then down and up the other leg.

Figure 8.3
Students moving mercury.
Constance and Amber start
with the mercury on the tip
of their left hand and slowly
start to move it along their
arm

Figure 8.4
Students moving mercury. As they move the mercury along their arms, they are thinking about the route it will take and how it feels as it passes through each muscle

Notes for the student

This exercise allows you to focus on movement passing through your body. As you practise this exercise, your movements will become more fluid and link together. Imagine an energy is travelling around your body and observe the effect it has on your body as you go through the exercise.

Student extension exercise: moving to music

Find a piece of classical music and do this exercise again, thinking about the mercury moving around your body while keeping in time with the music.

AS, A2, IB, BTEC National, GCSE, KS3.

52 COORDINATION

Student exercise

AIM

To work on coordination skills with a partner and as part of a group.

Paired exercise: removal men

- Imagine you are two removal men and have a large wardrobe to move out of the ground floor apartment on the street.
- Work together, keeping an impression of the size and weight, as you move the cupboard.
- Think about how you move, and the stresses the weight of the cupboard would have on you.

Lumberjacks

- Imagine you are two lumberjacks, the year is 1913, and you are sawing up a tree that fell down in last night's winds.
- It is a long saw, with a handle at each end, and about six feet long.
- Work on keeping the rhythm between you, and imagine the sawdust flying in the air as you work together.

House clearance

- You are two house clearers, Sue and Kate; your job is to go into a house, decide what objects are worth buying and load them on to your van.
- As each object is picked up, you discuss the worth and move it to the van. Sue, you initially pick up the items and then pass them to Kate to put in the van, all the time discussing their value and who would want to buy them.
- Anything worthless is thrown in the skip outside by Kate.
- As you handle each object, think about the size and weight and don't let the improvising of dialogue take you away from handling objects.
- If something is heavy, think about how you would pick it up and the tensions needed to handle it.

Group exercise: rowing team

- You are the British ladies coxless fours rowing team. You train every day together, and today there is a 5000-metres row on the Thames.
- Take your positions in the boat and take your lead from the front rower.
- Keep in time with each other and remember to imagine the oar going through the water and the strain on your chest, back, legs and arms.

British brickies

- You are a group of four bricklayers. You always work together and are known for your speed and your collective sense of humour.

- You are working on this house and are laying the outer walls. You all work in rhythm, passing bricks and tools to each other as you work.
- Remember to keep in mind the weight of the bricks in the hand, the feel of the cement on the trowel and keeping an eye on the time.

Notes for the student

With all these exercises, make sure you are imagining the weight and the effect this has on your body. It is about finding a happy medium between overdoing and underdoing the weight and strain. Let your imagination guide you and start to build up a muscle memory for different objects and sizes.

TEMPO-RHYTHM, VOICE AND MOVEMENT

Tempo-rhythm is our pace, both mental and physical, and the pace of everything around us and everything we do. Tempo-rhythm links the mind, body and spirit together in harmony. We have an inner tempo-rhythm and an outer tempo-rhythm.

The voice is one of the means actors have to communicate what their 'mind is creating clearly, deeply and invisibly'.[2]

The voice is an instrument that needs exercising in order to release its full capacity.

Our bodies enable the physical embodiment of the role, conveying 'the life of the human spirit'.[3]

'The body on display must be healthy, beautiful and in its movements expressive and harmonious.'[4]

For our bodies to express our inner workings, they must be flexible, strong and supple.

9 Rehearsing a play

This chapter will take you through the stages of rehearsing a play. You can use it as a step-by-step guide, or you may want only to do a few of the exercises. The last exercise is a fast-track path for you to follow. This is for the student with a short rehearsal period, preparing for auditions, or the teacher with limited time.

During the early years of his life, Stanislavski believed in having the actors around a table, pencil in hand, analysing and discussing objectives, actions, the super objective etc. In later years, Stanislavski favoured getting actors up on their feet and experiencing the role actively.

Students rehearsing a piece of text can dip in and out of this chapter throughout the rehearsal process, to support what is being done in your structured rehearsal time. If you are devising a piece of original theatre at A2, you can use the exercises to structure your rehearsals. If you are performing a piece of text or monologue/duologue, you can use these exercises to analyse the play. For the IB student, this chapter is useful for the units on 'Theatre in the making' and 'Theatre in the world'. If, for BTEC, you are examining how different practitioners rehearsed, this chapter outlines how Stanislavski rehearsed with his actors during the course of his life.

This chapter draws on Stanislavski's early and later years, giving you, the student, a rounded experience of Stanislavski to work through. For the various A level boards, you need to examine a practitioner, such as Stanislavski, and relate his work to a text. These exercises will allow you to do that fully. For BTEC students, you have to examine and work through rehearsal techniques and skills in 'Rehearsing for performance'.

If you are at drama school, university or rehearsing a play, you can work through these exercises to support the rehearsal process and help with the development of your character.

The rehearsal process is an opportunity for you to test out all the skills you have learned and to find out which areas of the system work best for you. It is a chance for you slowly to build, create and experience a character and ultimately let other people enjoy your creation. Audiences and examiners have one thing in common – they want to enjoy the play. If you enjoy rehearsing and performing, the chances are the audience will too.

AS, A2, IB, BTEC National, GCSE, undergraduate.

53 THE READ-THROUGH

Student exercise

AIM

To gain a valuable first impression of the play by reading it in a calm setting.

On your own

- When you know the play you are to be rehearsing, organize a time when you can sit down and read the play.
- Make sure you have two hours free of distractions.
- Relax your mind and start to read, remembering your impressions of the plot and characters as you go.
- When you finish, jot down your first impressions of the play and what you think the characters are like.
- It is these first impressions that will help start you on the road to analysing the play.

With the cast

- Sit around in a circle.
- Make sure that you have all read the play and thought about it at home.
- Read one of the parts, but don't try to perform it. You should read with the action 'I find out', trying to gain a totality of the play and the character.

Notes for the student

It's important to read the play for the first time with no distractions. Try not to rush through, but give yourself time to reflect on the play. If you know the character you are to play, try to read the play thinking about all the characters, and not just your own.

Notes for the teacher

I understand that it can sometimes be a struggle to get students (especially at the start of the AS year) to read the play they are working on. I have often run a workshop on a text where a couple of students are trying to 'get by' on what they have picked up from the back cover and a charming smile! Ask the students to read the play at home, and then the class read-through means you know that they have all read the play at least once. For the class read-through, don't allocate parts, but give them out at random. The students will then start to get an impression of the whole play and not just their character.

54 THE PLOT

AS, A2, IB, BTEC National, GCSE, undergraduate.

Student exercise

AIM

To clarify the plot to understand the storyline of the play.

- Once you have read the play, sit down and individually write down three or four sentences outlining the plot.
- In front of the rest of the cast, tell them (without reading out the sentences you have worked out) the main plot of the play as it appears to you.
- Now combine all your plots into one and you have the plot of the play.

Notes for the student

Remember, this is not an exercise about cutting and pasting from SparkNotes on the Internet. It is about you putting into your own words your impression of the play.

It is important for the whole cast to have a collective idea of the plot of the play before you start. Plays can mean different things to different people, so you all need to have a common understanding. It is best to do this at the start, so that you can build your analysis of the play from here. Stanislavski's actors used to tell their ideas on the plot of the play to the class. This often highlighted where students placed the most emphasis. For one person, Romeo and Juliet is a love story between two young people, whereas, for others, it is a story of family rivalry and revenge.

AIM

To clarify the
facts of the
play.

55 FACTS

Student exercise

- Go through the play, writing down everything you know to be true in the world of the play, any facts that the playwright gives that can be used.
- Write down the setting, ages, town names etc. for the play, and then any specific facts for individual characters.
- Now, work out the facts you do not know based on the ones you do. If the playwright does not give you a character age or how many siblings the character has, it's your job to work it out. Use the evidence of the play to guide you and help you come up with a decision. For example, if, in the play, a character has just left university, their age is likely to be 21. If the play is set in Ireland in the 1930s, you will probably have three or four brothers and sisters. Decide how many, their gender, ages and names.

Notes for the student

Students sometimes ask why we need to go into so much detail when working on a play. Everything you decide at this stage will have an effect on the character you create. If you make the character the youngest of three siblings, then their personality will be different from that of an only child. At university, I had a friend who was the youngest of eleven siblings; he had a razor-sharp wit and was a great show off. Logically, growing up as the youngest of eleven children, he had to be very vocal and develop a strong sense of humour to get any attention at all!

AIM

To clarify the
main events of
the play.

56 MAIN EVENTS

Student exercise

- Work through the play and write down all the main events that happen. The main events are the main things that happen in the play.
- Once you have the list, narrow it down to ten events, so that you can look at the play as a series of events that affect what the characters are thinking and doing.

57 RESEARCH

Student exercise

AS, A2, IB,
BTEC National,
GCSE,
undergraduate.

AIM

To find out information about the play, playwright, the period and the characters.

* You need to research:

    the setting of the play;
    the time of the play;
    the social, cultural, political events at the time of the play;
    information on the playwright and their life.

* Find images of the time, people, buildings and landscapes all unique to the period and country of the play. Go to the library and get out any books based on that time period. If there is documentary film available or old photos in books, have a look at them, or google images and see what comes up.
* As a cast, decide which images are the key buildings and locations in your play. If your play is set in a large house, decide which image best fits all your perceptions of the house.
* Find a map of the country the play is set in and locate the town or city where the action takes place. Make sure you know where it is in relation to other places mentioned in the play. If you don't know the town or city, decide on one that fits in with the play.
* Draw a map of all the surrounding area, so that you all have the same impression of the surrounding countryside and where things are. If, in the play, one character refers to the cherry orchard, you all need to know where the cherry orchard is, in what direction and what it looks like.

Notes for the student

If you are all working in a drama studio, you can put pictures and maps up on the wall to help trigger your imagination. If all the characters talk about 'the gardener' in your play, find a photo of someone who fits the gardener and put him on the wall. Then, the whole cast has the same image of the gardener. It is these little details that help to create a totality in the play. If all the cast members are imagining the same things, based on the same pictures, they will all have a real connection and communication on stage.

Performance tip

Use the research stage to build up pictures in your imagination of what things were like at the time of the play. The research stage is where you can discover some fascinating facts that will help in the creation of your character. Recently, I played a pilot, Captain Jack Alcock, the first man to fly the Atlantic. During my research, I found out that the plane he was flying was very difficult to control and laden down with gallons of fuel, water and oil. The strength needed to hold the plane steady during take-off was immense. The navigator later wrote that Alcock was white with the exertion of holding the plane during take-off. Armed with this information, I improvised the take-off at home, imagining trying to steady the plane during take-off, maintaining the tensions needed for such a task. This meant that, when filming the take-off, I would have all the information available to make the scene as realistic as I could.

AS, A2, IB,
BTEC National,
GCSE,
undergraduate.

58 THE BEFORE-TIME

Student exercise

AIM

To work out your character's before-time and present it to the cast.

- Think about your character's life, from their first memory to the start of the play.
- Think through the main events of your character's life, using your imagination actively to create real pictures and impressions of the character's past. Take a couple of minutes to think back over your own life and how many memories you have. Now do the same for your character.
- Sit before the rest of the cast and tell your character's story. Start with:

  I am . . .
  My first memory was . . .
  I have . . . brothers and . . . sisters.
  At five, I went to prep school in . . .
  At university, I studied . . .

Figure 9.1
Discussing a character's before-time. Constance is evaluating her character before-time for Nina in *The Seagull* (the 'Relationship' exercise in Chapter 5), saying what went well, what she missed out and what areas she needs to research further

• Work through your life like this, remembering to imagine the pictures actively, like a film reel before your eyes.

Notes for the student

When you are thinking back over your before-time, use the exercises from the chapter on imagination to make sure you are using all your senses. Often, a memory can be linked to a sense; the smell of the sea may take you back to a childhood experience. Imagine the events happening to you and what you felt about them. Use this actively to build your character. It is often the events of the past, and what we think about them, that affect what we want and think about in the present and the future.

Remember to incorporate into the before-time as much as you can to do with the events of the play. If you are playing Macbeth, you would want to imagine training, fighting, battles, meeting Lady Macbeth, becoming Thane of Glamis. You could also imagine a chance meeting with a witch as a young child and your fascination with what she said to you.

Rehearsal tip

Remember that the before-time is not just before the start of the play. If you go off stage and then come back on, you have to imagine everything you did in between for your re-entrance to be logical. If you are on stage and go off to go fishing, you, as the actor, need to imagine your character fishing and what you thought about it, so that, when you come back on stage, the audience understands where you have been and what you have been doing. Remember to use your imagination actively (refer back to Chapter 3 for some help with this).

Notes for the teacher

This exercise is a 'must do exercise' whenever working with students. It helps them to start to think about their character's past and how it affected the character. I ask students to go home and prepare their before-time and then check how much detail they have gone into when they present it to the class. If there is not enough detail, or they have not imagined the events actively, I talk them through creating the before-time in active imagination and ask them to give it another go. For example, if they are playing an American character, they will need imagined pictures of America for the audience to believe their character. If the play is set in Elizabethan England, they will need to imagine their before-time with pictures of the Tudor period.

AS, A2, IB, BTEC National, GCSE, undergraduate.

59 THE CHARACTER'S JOURNEY

Student exercise

AIM

To walk the character's journey through the play, working towards the 'starter' through action of the character.

- Start at the beginning of the play and walk through what your character is thinking through the play. Imagine the events happening and how you feel about them.
- Bring in an impression of your before-time while you are doing this, so you can start to combine the past with the present.
- Move on to looking at the major actions of your character through the various bits of the play and decide on the starter through action for your character.

60 SUPER OBJECTIVE AND GERM

AS, A2, IB,
BTEC National,
GCSE,
undergraduate.

Student exercise

AIM

To come up with a starter super objective and germ for the play and character.

- Referring back to Chapter 6 on the super objective and germ, as a cast, come up with a starter super objective for the play and a super objective and germ for your character.
- Remember these are only 'starters'; as you go through the experience of creating your character and working on the play, you will be able to fine-tune your original choices as you learn more about your character. In Figure 9.2, we see the actor at the start of the rehearsal process, with

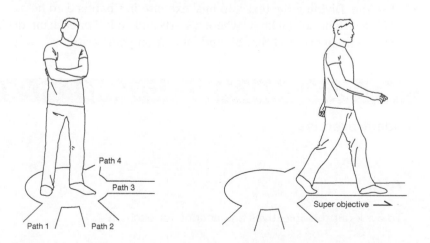

Path 4

Path 3

Path 1   Path 2

Super objective ——▶

Figure 9.2
Deciding on the super objective

a number of different paths to follow. By choosing one path, you give your character a direction to go in and a purpose to drive your character through the play.

61 RELATIONSHIPS

AS, A2, IB,
BTEC National,
GCSE,
undergraduate.

Student exercise

- Sitting around as a cast, work out the relationship that each character has with the others, what they really feel and think about each other.
- Use the 'Relationships' and 'Relationships 2' exercises in Chapter 5 to help.

AIM

To work out the character's relationships in the play.

Notes for the student

It is important for you to have a starting point to develop and work on your relationships with other characters. You may start with one impression of your relationship with another character and change it radically as you delve more into the subconscious of your character. This process is part of your character development and the discovery of the human spirit of the role.

62 DIVIDING INTO BITS

AS, A2, IB,
BTEC National,
GCSE,
undergraduate.

Student exercise

- As a cast, work through the play or section of the play, dividing it up into bits and giving each bit a number, starting at 1.
- Use the 'Dividing the text into bits' exercise in Chapter 1 to help.
- Mark each bit so you know where it starts and ends. For each bit, decide on the main event of that bit and label it on your script.

AIM

To divide the play into bits.

63 OBJECTIVES AND ACTIONS

AS, A2, IB,
BTEC National,
GCSE,
undergraduate.

Student exercise

AIM

To work out the objectives and actions for each bit.

Figure 9.3
Dividing the play into bits.
Amber is looking through a
section of Terry Johnson's
Hysteria ('Relationships 2'
exercise) to decide where a
bit will start and finish

- Go through each bit of the play, working out the objectives and the actions for each character.
- In your scripts, write down your objective and your action next to the main event for each bit.
- Use the analysis grid (Figure 9.4) so that you have a complete record of your journey through the play.
- In the final column, put into words your inner monologue. See 'The inner monologue' exercise in Chapter 6 for help.

Bit	Main event	Objective	Action	Inner monologue
1				
2				
3				
4				
5				
6				
7				
8				
9				
10				

Figure 9.4 Analysis grid

Notes for the student

Once you have completed the grid, go back and look at your character's super objective, through action and germ to see if they still work, and think about how you can update them. The grid means you can walk your journey from objective to objective, action to action, which will help the development of your character. You will also be able to see if an objective or action does not belong and stands out from the rest. It is a good idea to go back over Chapters 1 and 2 to remind yourself of the work done on objectives and actions. Don't forget to use your 'friend', the subconscious, to help guide you through this section. Stanislavski said that, to help us, we can 'throw a bundle of thoughts' into the subconscious and see what it produces.

The column for inner monologue helps you to put into the words of the character what you are thinking, as events happen.

Rehearsal tip

When annotating your script be as clear as possible, so use:

> I want to . . . for the objective
> I . . . for the action

Try not to write all over your script; you may have a couple of weeks' gap between the first time you look at a scene and the second time. Crisp, clear notes will jog your memory far more than a mini essay.

Notes for the teacher

You probably won't have time to do this exercise in class, so I suggest doing the first bit in class and then giving the rest as homework. Bear in mind that someone playing the lead will be in most bits and have a lot more work than someone who is only in a few scenes. You can take copies of their grids. Then, for each bit, you can prompt the students if they cannot remember their action or objective.

The fast-track option at the end of this chapter will give you the opportunity to fit this chapter into the time available. The students can always do the early stages at home and come in ready for Active Analysis.

AS, A2, IB,
BTEC National,
GCSE,
undergraduate.

64 ACTIVE ANALYSIS

Student exercise

AIM

For the student to use improvisation to analyse the bit and their character.

- Read a bit of the play and discuss what should be the main event for that bit.
- Discuss the given circumstances of the bit.
- Discuss each character's main action for the bit.
- Put your scripts down and improvise the bit using the given circumstance and action as your guide.
- Discuss how the scene went and if you felt the action fitted the scene. If it did not, change the action and re-read the scene.
- Start to discuss your objective, the relationship, the super objective etc. at this point. Your improvisations are the spark to ignite and bring together all the elements of the system.
- Improvise the scene again – don't try to remember the text, but concentrate on the action, objective and the given circumstance.
- Discuss the scene again and then read over the text. This process will start to see you combining the thoughts and actions of the character with the text. Each time you improvise, you will come closer to the text.

Notes for the student

Active Analysis means you are free to explore the action of the play and then add the text as you go. It frees you as the actor and means you do not have to walk the stage script in hand. By the time you sit down to 'learn your lines', you will realize you already know most of them. Because you understand what the character is doing and thinking, remembering the lines becomes a much easier task. The gelling of action and the text means that, when you start to think and move, the words will be there.

In his early days, Stanislavski analysed the play in depth, often around a table with the students visualizing the events of the play. Active Analysis saw Stanislavski getting the students up on their feet, exploring and experiencing their characters actively. A long analysis stage can often soak up the actor's inspiration for the role, and so getting straight in and working on your feet is a good way to harness your inspiration. In rehearsal, you explore and experience, and at home you evaluate and prepare for the next day.

Don't forget to use the other elements of the system that you have learned, such as free body, imagination and communication. Think back to the exercises you did on communication in Chapter 5; Active Analysis allows you to deepen the conscious and subconscious communication of your character with others on stage.

This way of working can be used with any text; even if you are doing a play largely using 'physical theatre', you can always use Active Analysis to structure and explore.

Notes for the teacher

Many of you will have a short amount of time to rehearse your sections of the play for public performance or to show a visiting examiner. Active Analysis allows you to get the students on their feet within the circumstances and 'giving it a go'. I would suggest getting the student to prepare the given circumstances and actions for each bit at home; you then discuss these as a group and start improvising. Then you evaluate, read the scene and then improvise again.

Active Analysis gets results and allows the student to create, without worrying about reading from the script. I try to make it as simple as possible. Once they know what is happening in the bit and have an action, I start the improvisation. It also means that, if a student dries or the lines go wrong in the performance, they can improvise their way out of the situation, getting back on track before the examiner/audience has had a chance to notice.

65 THE METHOD OF PHYSICAL ACTION

AS, A2, IB, BTEC National, GCSE, undergraduate.

Student exercise

* Decide on a bit from the play.
* Discuss the character's objective in the bit and then slowly walk through the physical actions of your character within that bit of the play.
* Discuss how walking through the physical actions started to inform your character's inner journey.
* Walk through the simple physical actions of the character for a second time, allowing them to inform the inner life of your character.
* Walk through the scene again, with the director feeding you your character's lines, which you then gel with the physical actions of the character.

- Analyse what your character was thinking and doing within the bit, as discovered through the physical actions of your character.

Notes for the student

By slowly walking through what your character is doing, you don't have to worry about what you are saying and you can concentrate on experiencing the subtext of your character as you walk through what they are doing within a circumstance. It often helps not to worry about the lines, but build what you are thinking and doing first, and then add the words later. I recently did a workshop on *Three Sisters* with a group of AS students; they were performing the play and had all learned the words and were busy acting the words at the expense of the subtext. I walked through several scenes with them, concentrating on the actions and what they were thinking and doing, so that they could then use that as a base for the words and not the other way round. The Method of Physical Action helps us to act what our characters are thinking and doing, rather than acting what our character is saying.

66 *MIS EN SCÈNE*

AS, A2, IB, BTEC National, GCSE, undergraduate.

Student exercise

> ### AIM
>
> To put the finishing touches and directorial vision to the organic rehearsal process.

- In your role as director, watch the scenes after Active Analysis and decide on any developments to the staging.
- Use the super objective of the play to guide you in how you direct the actors.
- Create your visual image that supports the logic of the play.

Notes for the student

You will work with a whole range of directors who will 'block' you in different ways. Some will tell you where to stand and when, whereas others will let you move organically and simply fine-tune these movements.

If you use all the exercises in this chapter, you should not need to ask 'what shall I do now', or 'where shall I stand'. From being in the given circumstances, with an objective and action, your movement will be organic. The process of Active Analysis means you have already moved around the stage and found your organic path. Then, if you are directed to move or sit or stand in a particular way, you can work backwards to create the inner and outer logic for the character within that circumstance.

Notes for the teacher

The reality will always be that some students will rely heavily on being told what to do on stage, whereas others allow the action and circumstances to guide them. Allow the student to explore first, and then guide them. If your time is limited, you might just need to 'direct' away, so that the students have a structure to work from. Remind the cast they need to provide their own character's logic to the mis en scène they have been given.

67 RUNNING THE PLAY

AS, A2, IB,
BTEC National,
GCSE,
undergraduate.

Student exercise

AIM

To polish and run the play for performance.

- Once you have actively analysed the play, do your first run of the play.
- After the run, go home and think through what went well, what you forgot, and what was not there that should have been there.
- For further runs, follow this process of evaluating after each performance.

Notes for the student

If a run goes well, remember to start again with the next run and not recreate what you did on the last run. The temptation may be to 'copy' what you did last time. Most actors at some point fall into this and can recognize when they are copying a previous performance, rather than experiencing it for the first time.

The idea behind running the play is to polish the play up to performance standard, so that you are no longer orientating as the actor but experiencing as the character. Always allow yourselves enough time to have a few runs and evaluation/notes sessions before you perform to an audience or examiner. There is nothing worse than going into a performance, knowing that you haven't run the play enough to make sure it has settled in your mind.

AS, A2, IB,
BTEC National,
GCSE,
undergraduate.

68 FAST-TRACK OPTION

Student exercise

- Read the play at home ('The read-through' exercise in this chapter) and work out the plot ('The plot' exercise) and the character before-time ('The before-time' exercise).
- Present your before-time to the class.
- Work through the play using Active Analysis (the 'Active Analysis' exercise), clarifying any facts (the 'Facts' exercise) as you go.
- Use the *'Mis en scène'* exercise in this chapter once all the lines have been learned. Then run the play ('Running the play' exercise).

Notes for the teacher

This fast-track option is for limited rehearsal time, so you can get the play up and running. However little time you have, I would suggest you work on at least the key scenes, using Active Analysis. This will help the student to create and experience their character. Use the exercises in this chapter to structure the students' work at home. You could spend the first five minutes of each lesson allowing students to feed back on what they did last night and how the exercises went. For those students who are less inclined to do the work at home, I remind them that, on the night, they will be on stage, in front of a couple of hundred people, and, as an actor, there is nothing worse than going on stage unprepared!

10 Improvisations

Improvisation is key to testing your skills and experiencing a character. You will put yourself in a given circumstance with an objective and action. You will use your imagination and have to check for tensions and relax. You will have an impression of your future, the super objective, and how to achieve it, the through action. You will respond to events, both expected and unexpected. You will need to communicate and identify the character's tempo-rhythm.

These improvisations are for you to combine all the skills you have been practising and use them together to create and experience your character. After each improvisation, think back and check what worked well and what did not. You may have 'dropped' your objective, or used a different action. With improvisations, you can also go again until you are happy.

Your time in training as an actor is ultimately about using the system to experience the role. Experiencing is where we allow all the work we have done to exist, and we 'let go'. We no longer think, 'what is my objective?', 'what is my action?', but allow them to be there, and we 'think' and 'do' as the character. Our thoughts and actions become spontaneous as the sub-conscious guides our character. Experiencing is where we leave the actor behind and find the character – with everything we do being the product of our character's thoughts and actions.

Recently, I was filming, and, when I arrived at the location for the morning's shoot, the director came over to me and the other actor and told us there was a problem with the location and we'd have to change the script slightly. Slightly meant completely, and we had all new lines and a new structure to the scene. The producer then came up to us and told us we didn't have much time at this location, so we needed to 'nail it' in a couple of takes. I had no real opportunity to go over the lines with the other actor and had to improvise and 'go for it'. I remember thinking, 'what do I want, how am I going to do it?' and then I heard 'ACTION'. When I saw the programme, I had expected my acting in the scene to be patchy; I was shocked when I watched the programme: this scene was by far the best acting. Because I was improvising, the scene felt alive and real – I was active in the scene. For this scene, I really experienced the role, with no choice but to put myself in the given circumstances and 'go for it'. All the work I had already done on my character was there, and my subconscious knew exactly what to do with it. It is our ability to be 'active', combined with the work already done on your character, that can produce real results.

One of Stanislavski's most famous pupils, Michael Chekhov, would improvise within the role without changing the text or the blocking. In this way, his character was alive night after night, as he experienced the role anew every time he stepped on stage.

Improvisation is the chance for you to 'let go' and experience the role. You are given a before-time and an objective and action. The super objective and germ will guide you in your future. You imagine these together, stand up and 'go for it'.

Do not think about what to say as the character; imagine the circumstances, your objective and action, and the words will come. If you try to force the words, they won't come; if you relax, they will start to flow!

AS, A2, IB, BTEC National, undergraduate.

69 BLIND DATE

Student exercise

Two-person improvisation, mixed gender

- Your name is Tom, you are 23, live in Barnet and work for *The Daily Mail*. You read psychology at Leeds University and are now living back at home with your mum while you get a deposit together for a flat. About six months ago, you split up with your long-term girlfriend and have not met anyone since. Your friends have recently been saying that you should get 'back out there'.
- Last week, you went out for a drink with a friend from university and his girlfriend. She told you that her best friend was single, gorgeous and looking to meet someone. After much brow beating, you agree to meet her. You are meeting outside a bar and have been waiting for about five minutes. You hear your name called and turn around to see your blind date. You enter the bar together and you go and buy the drinks. You sit down with the drinks, and this is where the improvisation will start.

  You have always gone out with quiet girls, the stay-at-home type. You like to go to the cinema and watch films at home. You've never been into the party scene, preferring a nice restaurant. Your blind date seems really boisterous and loud. She has already had a couple of drinks and called you 'Tommy baby'.

- Your objective is 'I want this over and done with', and your action is 'I look for a way out'. You know that you will have to stay for at least a drink, but have decided very quickly that this was a mistake, and you are trying to work out how to get out of the situation without offending her.
- Your name is Louise, you are 21 and from Gants Hill in Essex. You live with two other girls in a flat in Gants Hill and work for the Carphone Warehouse. You are the life and soul of any party. You go out four times a week and love clubbing. Your friend told you about Tom, saying he was a real catch: tall, dark, handsome and clever! Today being Friday, you went for a few drinks after work with the guys on your floor. If you like Tom, you are going to drag him to a club to meet your friends later. At work today, one of the guys locked the new guy in the stationery cupboard during lunch; you thought this was hilarious and, within seconds of meeting Tom, you recount the story. Tom has just gone to get drinks and you have decided that he is your type – handsome and mysterious. Your objective is 'I want to impress', and your action is 'I flirt'. While Tom is at the bar, you text your friend and check your make-up. You are now very glad you wore your mini and heels. One of your favourite songs comes on and you whoop at Tom and do your rave dance. He smiles back and you can sense he likes you.
- The improvisation starts when Tom returns with the drinks. Louise, you immediately start to talk about work and the laughs you and the guys have.
- You have the characters' before-time, given circumstances, objective and action. Imagine them while you prepare for the improvisation, and then give it a go.

Notes for the student

Remember, there is no right or wrong in the path you take during the improvisation, as long as it fits with the before-time, objective and action. Do not worry about what to say; allow the given circumstances and the action to guide you. After the improvisation, discuss the characters with the rest of the group, commenting on how the improvisation went and if the characters were as designed here.

Notes for the teacher

Give the students a minute to think about the improvisation before they go up to do it. Afterwards, let the audience comment on what they thought about the characters and if the actors had the objectives and actions designed.

Figure 10.1
Students in a workshop. Amber and Constance are having the 'Kylie is coming' exercise explained to them. I always imagined Stanislavski's rehearsal rooms to be a place of great practice and learning and also great fun and enthusiasm

AS, A2, IB, BTEC National, undergraduate.

70 KYLIE IS COMING

Student exercise

Three-person improvisation, mixed gender

- You name is Joe and you are the manager of a fashion boutique in Covent Garden. You are 32 and have worked in retail all your life. Your wife is a celebrity designer, and you stock a number of her designs. Yesterday, you got a call from Kylie's personal assistant saying that Kylie would like to have a look around your boutique. You have agreed to give Kylie free run of the shop from 11 to 11.30 tomorrow. You regularly meet celebrities at parties and functions with your wife and are looking forward to an endorsement from Kylie. This morning you ordered sushi (Kylie's favourite) and freshly squeezed orange juice. Kylie is due in around twenty minutes, and you want to make sure everything is ready. There are still a number of dresses in Kylie's size that need to be brought out. Your objective is 'I want to do my best', and your action is 'I look forward'.
- You are 16 and have just finished your GCSEs. You are working at the boutique over the summer and starting your A levels in September. This morning you came in to work as usual, and the manager told you that Kylie would be coming in at 11 o'clock. You have never met anyone like Kylie and you are not sure how you should behave. All morning

you have become more and more nervous and cannot stop watching the door. You want to play it cool, but are not sure how to be cool with Kylie. As 11 o'clock gets closer, you panic about what you're wearing and want to go out and get a new shirt. You ask the manager, and he tells you to get on with your work. You have checked your hair fifteen times already, and it's still not right. Your objective is 'I want to survive the encounter', and your action is 'I panic/I dread'.

- You are 24 and a senior sales assistant. You have worked in the boutique for about a year. You love clothes and fashion and spend all your disposable income on clothes. You have always got on well with Joe as your manager. A week ago, you were at an evening fashion show with Joe and you had a bit too much to drink. You got a bit loud, and Joe took you to one side and told you to behave professionally. Afterwards, you felt humiliated and, since then, have wanted to get back at him. When you hear that Kylie is coming in, you decide to take revenge on Joe; you don't want to lose your job, so you're going to have to be very subtle. Your objective is 'I want to get back at Joe', and your action is 'I plot/I scheme'.
- The improvisation will start with Joe, the manager, saying they have ten minutes before Kylie is due in and not all the dresses are out.

Teacher extension exercise: the PA arrives

After a few minutes, extend the improvisation with other characters. Kylie's personal assistant shows up with a problem, or a member of the paparazzi arrives, and Joe is worried that Kylie will think he called them.

71 THE BOOK CLUB

AS, A2, IB,
BTEC National,
undergraduate.

Student extended improvisation

Five-person improvisation, mixed gender

- Trish, you are 36 and unmarried. You host the weekly book club, every Thursday evening from 7 o'clock to 8.30. You have always loved reading; you read literature at university and take the book club very seriously. Your house is quite bohemian, with books and artwork from around the world covering the walls. You have written a novel, but it didn't do very well and went out of print quite quickly. You are trying to find a publisher for your second novel. You work in a bookshop, but mainly live off your inheritance. You set up the book club about a year ago, with a few friends. On average, you have five people attending, and you are always encouraging 'fresh blood'. Each week, one person chooses a book, and you all read it and then discuss it at the next meeting. Last week, you chose Life of Pi, by Yann Martel, and are quite desperate to share your thoughts on the symbolism of the novel. As the host of the book club, you are always anxious not to waste time on small talk and to use the time to discuss the book. This week, you have a new member of the book club, Tony. Your objective is 'I want to be special', and your action is 'I provoke interest'.

- Tony, you are 31 and an actor. You are friends with Sue, who comes to the book club, and have decided to try it out. About ten years ago, you were a regular in *Casualty*, but since then you have only picked up a couple of adverts and bit parts. You are a bit of a social animal and like nothing more than chatting the time away over coffee or a glass of wine. You haven't seen Sue for a while and see this as a good chance to catch up and have a moan about the lack of decent auditions. You read the book and think it was great, but you don't want to get too analytical. Your objective is 'I want to belong', and your action is 'I enjoy my time'.

- Sue, you are 28 and work in marketing. You have always read and have been a member of the book club since the start. You met Trish at the bookshop, and that's how you found out about the book club. This week has been one of the worst of your life. You have just split up with your fiancé; you were not going to come tonight, but have to because you have invited Tony along. You want to talk to people about what has happened and get their advice. You can't believe James, your fiancé, doesn't want to get married and wants to travel to Australia instead. Normally, you enjoy discussing the books and you get on well with Trish and Simon, but today you just want some care. Your objective is 'I want to be cared for', and your action is 'I pity myself'.

- Monica, you are 36, an American, you work in a merchant bank and see the book club as your creative outlet. In the bank you are referred to by the guys as a 'ball breaker'. You take no prisoners at work or in your social life. You tend to treat the book club as an extension of the workplace, a place to dominate and be respected. You think Trish is a bit of a hippy, and, although she may know books, she's too flaky to be taken seriously. Simon is like 'a wet weekend in Missouri' and just winds you up with his incessant drivel. You're divorced, twice, and have no time for relationships. Men are all the same and not half as satisfying as money. When it comes to discussing the novel, you see it like a meeting at work, where other people have opinions, all wrong, and need to be corrected. Your objective is 'I want to be superior', and your action is 'I provoke fear'.

- Simon, you are 25 and a librarian. You live at home with your mother and have done since you left school. You did not do well at school but managed to get a job as a junior librarian close to home. You have worked there for six years and feel quite secure in your work. You heard about the book club when Trish was in the library one day. You look up to Trish and really value her opinions on books. You're quite scared of Monica; she has a tendency to talk over you and call you derogatory names. You read the book several times during the week and jot down notes in your little book to read out during the book club. You always feel like you don't belong and try hard to be part of the group. Your objective is 'I want to be accepted', and your action is 'I drone on'.

- These are all starter objectives and actions that will probably change as events occur. Start with these and see what happens in the improvisation from the given circumstances and then evaluate and discuss it afterwards.
- Decide on your character's super objective, through action and germ based on the before-time given here.
- Think about the relationships you have with the others during the improvisation.

Notes for the student

After you have read the before-time for your character, work out the super objective, through action and germ of your character. Then imagine your objective and action and start the improvisation. When the improvisation comes to a natural conclusion, discuss how your objectives and actions changed as events occurred. For example, Sue revealing that her fiancé has left her and wanting to share this with the group would have an effect on all the others. You can then improvise the scene again, having discussed your new objectives and actions.

11 The acting exercise programme

This final chapter is to extend your skills and to cement all that you have learned and experienced. The exercises in this chapter are for you to work on alone and perform to others, whether in class or at home.

These exercises provide a link between your A level, IB or BTEC studies and university/drama school. They give you a programme that can be used in preparation for drama school auditions or university drama courses and throughout your higher education.

For the actor and student of acting, these exercises provide you with a programme you can work through when your skills need refreshing. For those of you back-packing around Asia on your year off, you may come back to an audition for a place at drama school and need to 'get back in the saddle'. These exercises should trigger any areas that need work, at which point you can return to the previous exercises in each specific chapter.

For today's actor, this chapter provides exercises to keep them finely tuned for the next audition.

For teachers, you may want to work the exercise programme into your schedule, to work on performance skills and give your students stage time in preparation for performing to a larger audience. The acting exercise programme would work in conjunction with the 'Theatre in the making' area of the International Baccalaureate Diploma.

AS, A2, IB, BTEC National, undergraduate.

72 VISUALIZATION 2

Student individual exercise

AIM

To chose an object and perform the object to an audience.

- Choose an object from the list of ten and work through the exercise.

Comb	Toothbrush
Book	Phone
Pencil	Door
Car	Lamp-post
Fridge	Catapult

- Imagine you are the object. Decide on where you are and how long you have been there.

  - What can you see? Imagine the view from where you are: does it change?
  - What can you hear?
  - What can you smell?
  - What can you feel?

- Imagine your past, the before-time and the events you have seen over the course of your life.
- Imagine your shape, size, texture, and position your body as the object.
- Decide on an objective and action.

Notes for the student

Rehearse by putting yourself in the best physical position for your object and visualize your life as that object. Remember to create pictures and images full of detail. If your object has working parts, you need to imagine them working and how they work. If you are made of steel, you need to imagine your body being that rigid and strong.

Rehearse a few times and then stand before your audience and see if they can guess what you are. Use the exercises and skills you've learned from the chapters on imagination and communication to help you.

Just think, if you can act a toothbrush or a lamp-post, you can act anyone!

73 THE ANIMAL

AS, A2, BTEC National, undergraduate.

Student individual exercise

AIM

To create the character of the animal and rehearse a short scene from the animal's life.

- Choose a wild animal. It can be any animal that lives in the wild.
- Research as much as you can about the animal: where it lives, what it eats, whether it is solitary or a pack animal etc.
- Find a few photos of your animal and watch a wildlife programme that features your animal.
- If possible, go to the zoo and observe your animal.
- Actively imagine the animal's past.
- Create your before-time as the animal.
- Decide on the plot of your short scene.
- Decide on the current given circumstances for the plot of your scene.
- Give yourself an objective and an action within that given circumstance and rehearse a short scene of about a minute long.
- Keep the plot, objectives and action simple. If you are a leopard, you may be stalking a prey. Or you may be an elephant keeping an eye on your calf.
- Think about how the animal moves and the tensions it uses.
- Imagine that your limbs are the animal's, so that you start to move like the animal and adopt the same physical characteristics.
- Remember, any physical characteristics must be linked to the inner actions of the character. If you, as a leopard, hunch your shoulders as you stalk, you need to decide why you, as the leopard, would do that. When doing your research, analyse why the animal you have chosen makes each movement.
- Rehearse the short scene a few times, working on the movement and keeping your objective and action in mind.
- Show the scene to your class or a friend to get their feedback. You can always film the exercise and watch it back and self-evaluate.

Notes for the student

This exercise tests your ability to combine the mental and physical. You will need to rehearse the movements of your animal thoroughly to get them right. The best way to do this is put yourself on all fours, think about how the muscles work as you move each limb and combine this with the physical characteristics of the animal. As you move, think about why you are moving, what you want to achieve and what you are doing to achieve it. If I am a leopard, my objective could be 'I want to bring down and kill the gazelle', and the action could be 'I stalk'. In this case, I would need to know exactly how the leopard hunts and kills its prey. Remember, if you don't do your research properly, it will be evident when you show the exercise.

74 THE CIRCUS PERFORMER

Student individual exercise

AS, A2, IB,
BTEC National,
undergraduate.

AIM

To create the character of a circus performer and design and perform a circus act.

- Choose a character who performs in the circus.
- Create the before-time for your character: where you grew up, how you ended up with the circus; include a few childhood memories that led your character to join the circus. If your character is a knife-thrower, then you could imagine that your father collected knives and, on Sundays, he would practise throwing them at a tree. Your character would watch with fascination as the knife flew through the air before imbedding itself in the tree.
- Research your character and the skills and training needed for your act.
- Decide on your character's super objective, through action and germ.
- Start to rehearse your act; decide on an objective and action, creating the given circumstances. You will need to design an impressive act to satisfy the audience, hungry to be amazed.
- Imagine what you can hear, touch, taste, smell and see. The circus big top will have very distinctive smells; you will hear music, children and families laughing.
- For this exercise, you will imagine you are performing in front of a packed house. Imagine the audience all around you and how you want them to react to your show.
- Rehearse your act several times; build in the interaction with the audience and others in the ring. If you are a lion tamer, you will need to imagine the lions and your relationship with them. You would train with them nearly every day and have a good understanding of their behaviour.
- You can start to think about your costume and, if you are showing your circus performer to the class, you can design and wear a costume.
- If you are showing your circus act to an audience, remember that, in the big top, there would be hundreds in the audience and music and clowns etc.

Notes for the student

Be creative with this exercise and really use your imagination. You could imagine the circus is in Turkey, and you are a Sicilian knife thrower. As the character, imagine an eventful past that led you to the circus. Create an impressive act that will thrill the audience. Think about how your character would use movement and voice to fill the whole big top. Enjoy the performance and enjoy the character; it's not every day you get to join the circus!

Figure 11.1

Watching an exercise. Amber and I are watching Constance perform an exercise; remember, you learn as much by watching others and evaluating their practice as you do working on your own

75 LIFE IN ART 2

AS, A2, IB,
BTEC National,
undergraduate.

Student individual exercise

- Look at Figures 11.2 and 11.3 and choose one of them.
- Decide on who you are, where you are, when you are living and your age.
- Research your before-time and find out details about the period and country you live in.
- Imagine the main events of your character's past, from their first memory to the day of the painting.
- Decide on a starter super objective, through action and germ for your character.
- Decide on the given circumstances of the character in the painting.
- Decide on an objective and action for your character, leading up to the painting.
- Devise a short scene that leads up to the painting and freeze in the final position. Include speech, either to other people or as a monologue.
- Think about how you are communicating throughout your short scene.
- Do your best to find the costume and props and then rehearse with these.
- Rehearse your scene several times over consecutive days; use your imagination during the rehearsal period to develop your character. Before each rehearsal, relax fully, using the 'Relaxation' exercise from Chapter 4.
- Show the scene to your class and evaluate how your acting was when performing the exercise on your own and when performing it to an audience.

Notes for the student

Remember to freeze in the final position of the painting. Ask a fellow student to check that you have ended up in the correct position. Use this exercise to work through the rehearsal process and to observe how you, as an actor, respond to performing in front of others. If you only have an audience of three people, it will still affect the performance. If you are on your year out before university or drama school, ask a couple of like-minded friends to watch and give feedback. Someone watching from the outside will often point something out that you had not thought about, which you can then go and work on.

Figure 11.2 (this page)
Lincoln the Railsplitter by
Norman Rockwell, courtesy
of The Butler Institute of
American Art, Youngstown,
Ohio

Figure 11.3 (facing page)
A Young Girl Reading by
Jean-Honoré Fragonard

AS, A2, IB, BTEC National, undergraduate.

76 MY FIRST CHARACTER

Student individual exercise

- Choose a character to be. It can be someone you walk past everyday, such as a waitress in a cafe, a policeman, a dentist or a builder.
- Start to imagine your before-time as the character; imagine where you live, your family and friends.
- Think about what you, as the character, do daily, from when you wake up until you go to bed. Walk through your character's routine as if it were your own.
- Decide on your super objective and germ.
- Put yourself in an everyday circumstance, give yourself an objective and an action and improvise a short scene a few times. If there is someone else in your scene, think about what your relationship with them is and how you communicate with them (through sending and receiving rays).
- Decide on your inner monologue for the scene and put it in the words of your character.
- Over the next few days, think about your character by putting yourself in your character's position. As you get dressed, imagine you are your character getting dressed, thinking about the day ahead. As you make a cup of tea, imagine you are your character making the tea and reflecting on the day you have had.
- Rehearse your scene again and then show it to your class or friends.
- Think about how you created and experienced your character 'on your feet'.

Notes for the student

For this exercise, do all your work on your feet, while you're waiting for the bus, brushing your teeth or getting dressed. Create and experience the character through 'being' the character and evaluate how effective this is for you.

I did an exercise similar to this at drama school, where the character I created was a Geordie sergeant-major working in an army stores, giving out kit to new recruits. I rehearsed my character by imagining working in the stores, with recruits coming in, and how I treated them. Today, I still use this exercise as a reference point for when I was thinking and doing as the character within a circumstance in active imagination. It means I have something to check my acting against when I'm not sure, in a new or challenging role. These exercises are designed for you to create an internal acting register that can be used throughout your career.

77 MASQUERADE

AS, A2, IB,
BTEC National,
undergraduate.

Student individual exercise

- Choose a character; it can be any character, ranging from a business-man to a peasant, a priest to an aristocrat, a heroin addict to an astronaut.
- Decide on your costume. If you have access to a costume room, browse through the costumes and find one that fits your character. You can visit charity shops for ideas, or ask at your local youth theatre or drama group for help.
- Think about the physical characteristics of the character – how the character walks, talks, sits, stands, moves etc.
- Once you have the costume and the physical characteristics, then put them to the back of your mind for a few days. Don't think consciously about your character; allow your subconscious to do the work for you.
- After a few days, put on your costume, do your hair/wig and start to walk and talk like the character. Put yourself in different circumstances and allow your imagination to guide you.
- For the next couple of days, put yourself in the character's position and improvise. Observe how your character develops and how the physical and psychological work together.
- Then, go in front of the class, fully made-up in your costume, and introduce your character and talk about yourself and your life. Stay in role and allow your character to develop.

Notes for the student

After you have gone before the class, think back over the whole process and how your character was created. How did your subconscious help during those few days. Often, our subconscious works for us. We throw in some ideas, and a few days later it's started to come up with a character. Remember that this is the last exercise in the book; if you were to do this at the start, your subconscious would not know what to do, but, over the course of the exercises in the book, you have been training your subconscious to work for you, when you need it. Physical characteristics can often be a very useful way into a character. You decide on a walk or a movement and then weave it into your character. On other occasions, you will be rehearsing, and a movement, a look or an inflection will just come to you and feel perfect for the character, and you will understand what it means to experience 'the life of the human spirit of the role'.

Afterword

Recently, I was in a shopping centre in Japan and, while waiting for my wife, sat down with my two children in front of a TV screen. Normally, baseball is being shown, but today they had a drama. The scene I watched involved a young guy, a young girl and her older friend. There was some kind of conflict, and they were walking along and discussing something. I speak no Japanese, so I sat and watched their acting. After a while, I turned to my son and said, 'It's as though Stanislavski never existed'. He smiled, nodded and said, 'Yes Papa' (my son is probably one of the only 4-year-olds to have named one of the cars he plays with 'Stanislavski'). I thought then how rare it is to see acting that has not been influenced by Stanislavski in some way.

For those three actors in Japan, somehow they had never encountered the Stanislavski system, and I thought how lucky we all are, as actors, to have had someone dedicate their life to giving us a system to use when acting that makes our job easier and clearer.

One thing I can safely say is that I am yet to meet a student whose quality of acting has not improved after they have been introduced to the exercises in this book. I have heard people say that the system is no 'silver bullet', no guarantee of success. However, give me the exercises in this book, a group of students for four hours and a nice, warm drama studio, and I can guarantee they will come out better actors, with a better understanding of how to use Stanislavski in their text or devised work than they had before.

So now, it's over to you; in this book you have a range of exercises on which to build your practice; now, all you need is some hard work, dedication and a sense of humour, and I'll see you at the Oscars!

Glossary of terms

action
What we do, as the character, to fulfil our objective.

Active Analysis
A rehearsal technique where actors analyse a bit of the play 'on their feet'. The actors decide on the main event, an action for each character, and then improvise that bit.

active imagination
Seeing things through our character's eyes, using the five senses.

before-time
The events leading up to the start of the play, or before each new entrance your character makes. Your character's life imagined actively from your first memory up to the start of the play.

bit
A play is divided up into manageable sections or units by the actors and director. A bit starts when there is an event on stage, the character's objectives change or a character enters/exits.

communication
The sending out and receiving of signals between two living beings.

event
Something that happens that affects what you are thinking and doing.

experiencing
The state where you leave the actor behind and find the character, with everything you do being the product of your character's thoughts and actions.

free body
The desired state for an actor, a body free from tension, which can be used to create and experience a role.

germ
The essence or seed of a character.

given circumstance
The situation the character is in within a particular bit of the play.

imagination
The ability to treat fictional circumstances as if they were real.

inner monologue
The thoughts going through our character's mind.

objective
What we, as the character, want to achieve within a given set of circumstances.

magic if
The question, 'what if', that the actor asks themselves to trigger the imagination within a given set of circumstances.

passive imagination
Seeing ourselves from the audience's point of view while on stage.

psychophysical
The combination of what we are thinking and doing that works across the system. What we think and do working together in harmony.

rays
An invisible current that flows between us all the time.

relationships
The thoughts we have about others.

subconscious
The part of the mind that influences our thoughts and actions without our being aware of it.

super objective
The theme of the play, the sum of all the objectives of the characters; it's what the play is really about. For a character, the super objective is what they want over the course of the play.

tempo-rhythm
Our pace, both mental and physical, the pace of everything around us and everything we do.

through action
What the character does to achieve their super objective.

truthful
Acting is truthful when, based on a set of given circumstances, you are thinking and doing as the character, imagining actively with a free body and a clearly walked through before-time.

visualizations
The pictures we see in our mind's eye.

Index of terms and exercises used in this book